Letters & Diaries of Lady Durham

Edited by Patricia Godsell

ISBN 0 88750 323 3

Cover portraits of Lord and Lady Durham by Sir Thomas Lawrence, courtesy the Public Archives of Canada. Editing by Sally Eaton. Book design by Michael Macklem.

Printed in Canada

PUBLISHED IN CANADA BY OBERON PRESS

Lady Durham

Despite the fact that she was the eldest daughter of Earl Grey, Prime Minister of Great Britain from 1830-34, was married to one of the most flamboyant political figures of the time and possessed remarkable beauty and charm, Lady Louisa Lambton, second wife of John George Lambton, 1st Earl of Durham, always remained a quiet and unassuming person.

Lady Louisa had come of age when London society was still noted for the exuberance of its fashionable life and for the brilliance of its hostesses. Queen Victoria had not yet ascended the throne, and it was still many years before Prince Albert was to arrive in England and cast his reproving, Lutheran eye upon the extravagances of the English aristocracy.

In 1816, when Lady Louisa Grey married John George Lambton, the drawing rooms of Mayfair and the great country houses were still the centres of a society that refined its pleasures into an art, including that particular pleasure that comes from the manipulation of power into a formidable weapon. In such an arena a fashionable hostess could wield a dangerous whip.

But neither in London, where her husband played the most controversial political game of them all in his support of the Radical wing of the Whig party, nor at the famous court of St. Petersburg in Russia where he was sent as Ambassador, nor in Canada, where he arrived with great pomp as Governor General of British North America, did Lady Louisa attempt to assume such a role. Quietly and graciously, she devoted herself to giving him her constant support and encouragement while keeping herself always in the background.

Certainly it could be said that in one family there would have been no room for another ambitious extrovert of the calibre of Lord Durham himself. But had she so wished, as many another woman of her time had been known to do, she could have exploited his position and notoriety for her own ends.

In the first place this was not in her nature, and in the second, her husband himself was the focus of her life. Louisa Durham was essentially a private person who lived almost solely for her family, at the very centre of which was John George Lambton, the man and the politician—"Him," as she refers to him so often in her journal, in almost reverential terms. Not only did she obviously adore him, but she was also his most ardent admirer and loyal supporter—and, by reason of her, he was one of the most fortunate of men.

In other respects Lord Durham can almost be considered a tragic figure—in the classical sense of possessing that flaw of character that makes a man his own worst enemy and finally destroys him, and in the sense that, in spite of his great achievements, other circumstances intervened and distorted his successes to such an extent that even history has not given him his just reward. Certainly in Canada he is thought of principally—understandably so perhaps—as the arch enemy of the French Canadians, the figure possibly beyond all others who is blamed for thwarting their aspirations to complete equality with English Canada. In Britain he tends to be remembered as a bombastic, hot-tempered, opinionated Radical who caused Lord Melbourne undue trouble as he attempted to keep his tottering government in power. Yet Lord Durham was one of the founders of the democratic system of government. His vision allowed the Empire, and later the Commonwealth, to develop as a remarkably peaceful relationship between a diversity of peoples. And it was he who set the seal on Anglo-American friendship.

Few historians have really looked closely and objectively at the final stage of Lord Durham's career—the Mission to Canada that brought about his downfall—in the context of his relationships: with the Melbourne government which dared not offend its right-wing element; with his Tory enemies who were hotly opposed to any extension of the franchise or loss of direct control over the Colonies; with his Radical rivals—particularly Lord Brougham whose personal vindictiveness was the final cause of

Durham's defeat. Because of its far-reaching consequences, his *Report* still stands out as a milestone in Colonial history. But the facts surrounding the Canadian Mission are frequently swept under the carpet.

In Britain, this final debacle of Durham's, has usually been seen from the point of view of Whitehall. Sympathy has been largely directed toward Lord Melbourne, who quite openly detested Lord Durham—they were complete opposites in temperament.

For Melbourne has been considered as having little choice in the difficult situation he had to deal with. He has generally been depicted as the quiet, rational, gentleman-politician, faced with the delicate task of keeping his government afloat on the stormy seas of internal political intrigue, not of his choosing nor to his taste. Ireland, Canada, the Radicals, the Tories: all were thorns in Melbourne's long-suffering side. But Durham was the last sharp straw—a bounder, and a persistent one.

In Canada, Durham has received a much fairer hearing— particularly in the excellent biography written of him by Chester New, now, sadly, out of print. New made no attempt to gloss over Durham's unfortunate personal weaknesses—and undoubtedly his pomposity, his tactlessness, and his outbursts of temper caused him, and his efforts, to be judged harshly by many people. Chester New also emphasized his strengths and gave him the credit for the outstanding achievements that frequently appear to have been interred with his bones.

Perhaps the tragedy of Durham's character was that to an even greater degree than is the case with the majority of men, his personality was split into so many diverse and contending forces. He was an aristocrat who worked tirelessly for democratic reform. He was a man of great vision; yet few could be so petty. His tact and good manners with Canadians of both cultures, and with the many Americans he met during his term of office in Canada, was widely remarked upon. But he could be outrageously rude to his colleagues. His patience and consideration for detail in his negotiations for a settlement between Canadians of different factions, and in his understanding of their

7

problems with Whitehall, was remarkable. Yet his impatience with what he considered stupidity or stubbornness often caused him to make rash and foolish remarks and ill-considered judgments. His personal courage reached levels of heroism, particularly in his determination to conquer the constant physical illness and pain that he suffered all his life.

Death was no stranger to Durham. His first family all died of tuberculosis: his wife within three years of their marriage, two of their daughters in their teens within six months of each other and the third at the age of 22. The crowning blow was the loss of Charles, his eldest son by his second marriage, who, at the age of thirteen died of the same disease. Each death caused him untold grief, but each time he pulled himself out of despair and returned to his political battles, until finally he, too, died of tuberculosis, complicated by his other chronic illnesses, at the young age of 48. Strangely enough, despite this remarkable courage in the face of illness and death he was liable, at certain moments of stress, to succumb to complete psychological collapse, as if in the ultimate test, his apparent enormous self-confidence crumbled and he lost faith in his own opinions. Evidence of this is clearly seen in two letters written at the time of the final crisis by Charles Buller, his principal adviser on the Canadian Mission. One was addressed to Durham himself and the other to John Stuart Mill. Further support is given in a letter from Col. Charles Grey, Durham's brother-in-law, to his father, Earl Grey (see note 102).

This book consists of a journal written in 1838 by Lady Durham, interspersed with a series of her letters to her mother, Lady Mary Grey. These give personal testimony to the events that occurred from the time that it was suggested that Lord Durham should go to Canada as Governor General to attempt to settle the problems that had led to the uprising of 1837, until his return to England in December 1838.

Lady Durham was not, of course, an unprejudiced or detached observer of the events that took place. However her facts and her general account of the progress and success of the Mission, coincide consistently and accurately with those from other contemporary sources. Moreover, although she was devoted to her husband, Louisa Lambton was the daughter of Earl Grey, who was known for his fastidious and moderate nature. He quite openly disagreed with his son-in-law's more radical views, and often deplored his volatile personality. Lady Durham, herself the link between the right and left wings of the Whig party, was not ignorant of her husband's difficulties, but she was also acutely aware of the injustices done to him by his own government on the Canadian issue. Apart from his wife, only the other members of Durham's staff, particularly Charles Buller, were able to appreciate fully the unwarranted viciousness of the attacks made upon him by his enemies in London, and the shabby way in which he was eventually abandoned by Lord Melbourne and his ministers.

What emerges from Lady Durham's journal and the letters that supplement it, is a most moving human reaction to an almost hopeless situation—a sense of frustration and indignation over circumstances that should have brought nothing but credit to her husband. In fact, the situation brought public disgrace to him in England, the formal disapprobation of the Queen and, in their contempt of the British government, the reactivation of the forces of rebellion in Canada.

A brief outline of the situation in Canada in 1838, of the problems that Durham had to face, the solutions he attempted and the results that ensued, may help to give a general context for the reading of the journal. As well as Lady Durham's own comments, the notes that are appended and the more detailed account given by Charles Buller in his *Sketch of Lord Durham's Mission to Canada in* 1838 (P.A.C. Durham Papers, No. 23, Vol. 1) that appears as an appendix should give a much clearer understanding of the actual situation from the viewpoint of those directly connected with the Mission.

In 1837 rebellion had broken out in both Upper and Lower Canada. Certainly the racial tension between the French and the English in Lower Canada was a major factor in the uprising in that area—the conflict between the basically agricultural French and the mercantile British simmered continually. The cause in the Upper Colony, and an aggravating factor in the Lower one, was the friction arising from the form of government imposed by the British in the Constitutional Act of 1791. Under this act each colony was administered by a governor appointed by the British government and advised by an Executive Council and a Legislative Council, both appointed by the Governor himself. The Legislative Assembly was the only elected body and it was consistently overruled by the combined power of the Governor and his supporters, known in Upper Canada as the Family Compact and in Lower Canada as the Château Clique.

There were additional causes of discontent in each province, but the major issue that bound together the rebels of Upper and Lower Canada was the question of effective representation.

In March 1838 Lord Durham was appointed Governor General of British North America. Over and above this he was given full administrative powers in Lower Canada, where he took over from Sir John Colborne who had been acting as Governor after the resignation of Lord Gosford. In Upper Canada and in the Maritime colonies the Lieutenant Governors were retained.

In a letter to his father-in-law, Lord Grey, he wrote:

I have stipulated with Melbourne that it is to be a temporary mission. I am not to be stinted in powers or in money and am to have unstinted appointment of all civil officers whom I may think necessary for the efficient execution of my duties. The undertaking is a fearfully arduous one and nothing but the extreme urgency of the case could induce me to make such a sacrifice both public and private (Howick MSS, 15 January, 1838).

In his reply to Durham's reluctant acceptance of the post, Lord Melbourne wrote to him:

I can assure you that I consider you as making a great sacrifice for the chance of doing an essential service to the country. As far as I am concerned, and I think I can answer for all my colleagues, you will receive the firmest and most unflinching support (Lambton MSS, 5 January, 1833).

From the start the Mission was plagued with problems originating in London, most of them arising from criticism levelled by members of his own party. He was given vast powers, but in the words of Sir Charles Lucas (*Lord Durham's Report*, Oxford, 1912): "It would be difficult to find a more futile set of instructions to a strong man setting out on a difficult mission, but they had the merit of leaving him a wide discretion." Ironically it was this that brought about his downfall.

In Canada itself the Mission started well. In order to make a clean start Durham appointed a Special Council in Lower Canada consisting of members of his own staff, to replace the old Executive Council. He issued a proclamation in which he invited "free unreserved communication" and showed a sincere desire to resolve the disagreements that were dividing the Canadas. He took a firm line over a recent act of piracy by a group of American citizens who were aiding the Canadian rebels, and offered a handsome reward for their capture. At the same time he sent a special delegation to Washington, headed by his brother-in-law, Col. Charles Grey, to heal the differences that were threatening a fresh outbreak of hostilities between Canada and the United States.

Since the end of the War of 1812 there had been frequent hit-and-run skirmishes across the border by unofficial American supporters of Canadian independence. After the 1837 rebellion many Canadian rebels had fled to the States where they were attempting to find support for renewed resistance. The American government, though under increasing pressure from "sympathizers," was reluctant to be dragged into further disputes and welcomed Durham's timely and cooperative delegation.

Durham's tact and courtesy to visiting Americans and Canadians of all factions—in spite of the fact that he was a quick-tempered and impatient man—made a great impression on all those who came into contact with him. In short, during the four months that he was in Canada he had remarkable success in personal diplomacy. He also gave clear evidence, by instituting Commissions of Inquiry into the most sensitive areas of administration, that he intended to dispose of the outstanding causes of dissension. Ironically enough, his adversaries at the time were neither the English nor the French in Canada, but colleagues in London, of whom the most scheming and vindictive was Lord Brougham, a former friend and fellow Radical with whom he had quarrelled. Numerous minor matters were criticized, and finally Brougham and his supporters found a legal technicality by means of which they succeeded in bringing Lord Durham down.

One of the most urgent and delicate problems that Lord Durham had to face on his arrival in Canada, was how to deal with the political prisoners arrested during the rebellion of 1837. Nearly 500 had been seized and about two-thirds of these had subsequently been released. The difficulty with the remaining third was that if they were brought to trial in Lower Canada, 'French Canadian juries there would acquit them. Durham refused to pack the juries to avoid this, but he also felt it unwise to sign a general amnesty for some of the prisoners were serious troublemakers. Lord Durham solved the problem with a decision that was accepted with general approval in Canada. In his ordinance, the eight principal leaders were banished to Bermuda, on pain of death if they returned. The remaining 153 were released. This was better than the French Canadians had hoped for, but at the same time the ringleaders were removed from the scene.

In the House of Lords, however, Lord Brougham vigorously protested the illegality of this action. He argued that the eight men could not be banished without trial, nor could Durham properly threaten them with death if they should return to their own land. Though Durham's original commission had given him virtually unlimited powers, and though it was generally agreed —even by the Prime Minister, Lord Melbourne—that his decision was a sensible one, unless the government was prepared to pass supplementary legislation to justify it (which they refused to attempt, as they feared defeat in the House), the illegality of Lord Durham's ordinance could not be denied.

He had no choice but to resign. In spite of a wave of support for him in all parts of Canada, and from many people in England, his authority had been completely undermined and, beyond some weak attempts in his defence, his Government abandoned him. Lord Melbourne disallowed the ordinance.

It was with great bitterness that Durham left Canada with his work still unfinished. Two years later, at the age of 48, he died. Lady Durham survived him by only sixteen months.

"Durham's *Report* was written in England in the two years before his death. Unfortunately, one aspect of the *Report* tends now to overshadow all the rest. Perhaps because of the shortness of his stay in Canada, perhaps because of prejudiced advice given him by Ellice and the British mercantile group, Lord Durham never understood the needs and desires of the French Canadian population, or if he did, failed to realize the implications of denying them. Whatever his reasons, the results were disastrous. His insistence in the *Report* that the French Canadian identity must be obliterated and that Canada must become an English nation in all its parts has led to nearly 150 years of tension. In other respects however, the *Report* was one of the most farsighted and prophetic documents in the history of this country, paving the way for responsible government, for Confederation and for Canadian independence" (Introduction to *The Diary of Jane Ellice*, edited by Patricia Godsell [Ottawa, 1975], p.16).

The concluding words of Lady Durham's journal, written after their return from Canada are:

> He was not able to take part in the Session of '40, but He saw the triumph of his views for Canada, & could foresee the success of His principles. Justice is as yet imperfectly done to Him, at least in England, but the time may come when He will be better appreciated.

Curiously enough the Lambton family motto is "Le jour

viendra." Unfortunately, as yet, history has not really vindicated Lord Durham, either in Canada or in Britain. Certainly the effects of the *Report*, in constitutional terms, stand as his greatest monument. Historians and scholars of political science remember him also for his contributions toward great reforms in suffrage and the alleviation of religious discrimination. But in the context of the nineteenth century as a whole, he still tends to be remembered as an *enfant terrible* who wildly rocked the boat, while in Canada he was recently included in a newspaper poll as one of the Five Most Unpopular Men in the nation's history.

Lady Durham's journal, which was started in January 1838 and closed in December of the same year was published as a typescript print-out in a limited edition by the Literary and Historical Society of Quebec in 1915. (This institution stopped publishing in 1927). The typescript was acquired by the Public Archives of Canada in 1938 from Lady Doughty, widow of Sir Arthur Doughty, Dominion Archivist 1904-35. A. G. Doughty, in his own handwriting, attested to the accuracy of this transcription, but the location of the original (despite a long search) and the date of the transcription, are not known. The present Lambton family did not know of the existence of Lady Durham's Canadian journal, and it has not been published in Britain.

Lady Durham's letters to her mother, Lady Mary Grey, written just before and during the visit to Canada, together with a few after their return to England, are from the collection of the Durham MSS held by the Lambton family. They have never before been published in their entirety. Their value, despite the disadvantage of some repetition of the journal, lies in the way in which they enlarge upon the diary entries and in their spontaneous, personal quality. Only two letters, those of 27 May and 5 June, 1838, have been excluded, as they add nothing further to the journal material for those days: and half of the first letter of ? January, 1838 has been omitted as its purely personal content would be of no general interest.

Very few editorial changes have been made in the original texts and the transcription of the handwriting has been done as faithfully as possible. Minor updating of punctuation has been made. Occasionally an entry has been brought under a specific date, which had been omitted as a heading, or was unwieldy, because many days' entries had been combined.

The notes that are given as an appendix at the end of the book are intended to serve two purposes. Firstly, their aim is to give additional information on the individuals, places, events, etc. that are referred to in the journal and letters. Secondly, the material provided is intended to give factual corroboration to many of Lady Durham's statements. Charles Buller's *Sketch*, which forms an important appendix, gives a detailed outline of each stage of the Mission, from its planning to its conclusion, and his own opinion of the conduct of the whole affair. Though, like Lady Durham, he was not, of course, an objective bystander, he *was* present at the Canadian end, and therefore his views are necessarily different from the accounts given by his contemporaries who remained in England. I have also included copies of letters written by Charles Buller to Lord Durham, and to John Stuart Mill, and others from the Prime Minister, Lord Melbourne and Lord Glenelg (Secretary for War and the Colonies) and also one from Queen Victoria to Lady Durham. Many comments made by Lord Durham's brother-in-law, Col. Charles Grey, who was in Canada at the time, in his personal journal and in letters to his father, Earl Grey, are mentioned. Some contemporary newspaper articles and other relevant material are also attached.

I am most grateful to Lord Lambton, Lord Durham's present heir, for his generosity in permitting me to study the family documents in his possession and for giving me permission to publish them. I would also like to thank Miss Hester Borron, Archivist of the Lambton collection, for her kind cooperation and for the amount of time she has spent assisting me to gather the material I have needed.

The Public Archives of Canada have been most generous and efficient with their assistance over permission rights, photocopying and photography. Miss Pat Kennedy, Pre-Confederation Archivist, has been exceptionally helpful, thorough and considerate with all my many requests and I would like to thank her particularly.

PATRICIA GODSELL

The superior figures in the text refer to the notes, which follow the text of the letters and diaries.

Letters & Diaries

The proposal of going out to Canada as Governor General was first made to L[ambton][1] in the summer of 1837. He then refused, but news of the Insurrection[2] having been received towards the end of the year, the application was renewed.

[However] he was induced after great difficulty & much solicitation to give in his consent, which he did Jany. 16th 1838, & it was agreed that he should sail for Quebec at the end of the Spring when the navigation of the St. Lawrence would be open. We then passed above three months in London occupied with the preparations of our departure. The doubts & fears belonging to the Undertaking & the regrets at again leaving home (having so recently returned from Russia) seemed continually to increase in this long interval of expectation, & the parting from those we left in England was most painful.

Thursday, ? January 1838

My dearest Mary,[3]

Many, many thanks for your letters, but I am beginning to think after all the pains we have been taking to reconcile ourselves to the Canada expedition, we may perhaps not be called upon to make any efforts on the subject. The matter seems very hard to settle. I hear of nothing but disputes and disagreements of which I cannot pretend to judge, & nobody seems confident of a majority for ministers in the H. of Commons. I suppose it is wrong not to wish for them more cordially, but I cannot help feeling that I could not lament if they were turned out, and we were saved from such an undertaking....

Pray give my best love to Papa,[4] *Georgiana,*[5] *& good bye my dearest Mary.*

Yr. most affect.
Louisa[6]

My dearest Mary,
I have been so taken up all day that I have not had time to write,
but now that we have done dinner & that Lambton is gone to the
H. of Lords I can just send you a few lines. I set out with Mary[7]
at 12 *o'clock for her first sitting to Mr. Ross,*[8] *who kept her* 2
hours, & when I came home I found we were to dine at 4. *I was*
not very sorry to have been away, for I do not feel in a humour
to see any body & am provoked at the comfortable contented
way in which people seem to consider our expedition. I believe
that there is nobody but you who will really care for our going,
& Lambton is becoming so excited about it, that I hardly dare
appear before him in a grave face, and yet, tho' I do not spare you
I should think it very wrong to give way to any unreasonable
grief on the subject, it is impossible *I should not feel many a*
bitter pang & many a heavy anxiety when I consider our pros-
pects. Sir G. Grey[9] *dined here yesterday, & it seemed to me from*
the way he spoke, that they would be much inclined to hurry us
away earlier than they need. This however Lambton will resist
& will not *go away till April which is quite soon enough, as the*
St. Lawrence is not open till May. Mr. Ellice[10] *encourages him*
to this, & I must own is very good natured to me, he wishes his
son[11] *to go—but this is a secret at present on account of his seat in*
Parlt—but he would not proceed upon the matter until he had
consulted me, as to whether I should like having Mrs. E.[12] *I*
attested very cordially for all I hear she is very amiable & I hope
she will be a resource to us all. Lambton told me yesterday what
he had said to Papa & in one thing I must confess I could not
agree. I would not lift a finger to help the Govt. but when one is
told that one may be the means of doing much good & of pre-
venting much bloodshed in an unhappy country, then I think it
is difficult to refuse ones best exertions, & if the thing succeeds I
shall rejoice on this account, but not at all for the sake of the
Govt. I feel a wicked wish to say this to all of them, & have done
so to Mr. Ellice and Mr. Ponsonby,[13] *but I suppose, even if I*
have the opportunity, that I may as well hold my tongue with

the others.

I have seen Caroline[14] *& her children, & was delighted to find Charles looking so well. He is grown quite fat & altogether looks clean & healthy.*

I must now, my dearest Mary, put up my letter but pray give thousands of loves to Papa. Mary sits again to morrow so that again I may be hurried but I will write when I can.

Yr. most affect.
Louisa

Alice[15] *was sitting by me yesterday when I was reading your letter & she is just beginning to be able to make out writing, which is a great pleasure—she reads over me "my beloved Louisa"—she said instantly "I am sure that is Gd. Mama," I asked her why & she answered she was sure it was you who called me "beloved." I thought this very pretty of her.*

Cleveland Row
Saturday

My dearest Mary,
I had begun writing to you yesterday but was interrupted & I am not sorry, for I have more comfort in answering the letter I have received from you this morning. It must always be, my dearest Mary, a most serious grief to me to be separated from you & the separation is now aggravated by the distance & the circumstances of the case, but I am much more miserable when I think that you are given up to the dismal forebodings you have mentioned. It is a most anxious undertaking certainly, & I feel so indolent in spirit, that I wish for nothing but peace & quiet, but I am determined to endeavour to hope for the best & to listen to such favorable accounts as do not appear unreasonable. My first & greatest anxiety will be about health, & if Lambton & the children can only return without having suffered, I shall consider myself quite happy—if also Lambton should succeed in his mission I do not pretend to say it will not be an immense satisfaction but even should he fail I should not be unhappy, & I hope he would be able to comfort himself with the reflection of

19

having acted conscientiously for the best. All human quests are subject to failure & beyond our control, but I hope he is as likely as any one to behave with prudence & judgement, & if the country is to be saved he will deserve the credit of it, tho' he ought not to be blamed for the reverse, having had nothing to say to the measures which have brought about the present crisis.[16] *I am most anxious to see you but the weather is so cold that I would not for the world that you should think of travelling till it changes. Mr. & Mrs. Ellice do go with us & Edward is to undertake the whole management of the house which is the greatest possible comfort to me. We are to have a Housekeeper who will have to do with me, but every thing else & every expense is to be managed by him. He has already entered upon his office, & I hope we will be able, before we go, to get the better of the smothered flames which I believe still exist in the house.*[17] *I have got the picture of Gd. Mama, it had been put by, by mistake, but I enquired for it & found it some time ago. The children & Lambton all desire their love to you. Alice says she has not forgotten you at all & hopes she never will. We are very impatient to know whether Harry*[18] *will be able to come with us. Pray give thousands of loves to Papa, Georgiana—& goodbye my dearest Mary.*

Yr. most affect.
Louisa

Charles[19] *has not given up all thoughts of going & I believe he might be allowed to keep his Equerryship, but he has a great deal to consider about his regiment.*

Monday 15th

My dearest Mary,
Your letter is much what I expected to receive & tho' I will hope it may not be as bad as we expect, still there is quite enough in such an undertaking to make one very unhappy. Do not however, my dearest dear Mary, talk of a final separation from you and Car[20]*—such a thought I cannot endure for one instant. Car is, thank God, well & strong, & if I did not think I should find you*

both still little changed at the end of the year & a half, I should be miserable indeed. This absence at such a distance & in such circumstances is bad enough, but it cannot & must not last longer. Ld. Melbourne even says that if by any good fortune the measures they propose should be adopted & arranged by this next Autumn that Lambton might then return himself with the agreement. This however, I suppose, is scarcely possible, but by the Autumn after, every thing must be decided one way or the other & he will return. It is positively to be considered a temporary mission, so much so that Ld. M says I need not give up my appointment[21] tho' on the first view of the case I had thought it might be an opportunity of getting rid of it, on further consideration I think it is better to retain it, in order to keep up every appearance of the absence being a temporary one. As to my dear Mary, I am quite sensible of the disadvantage to her—that & the separation from you are the two points which press upon me most. I hope the climate will not prove injurious & I hope & trust Lambton may succeed in pacifying the country, but if he does not it will be the height of injustice to impute the failure to him, & I should think it would be almost impossible to do so after the state in which the country has been left, & as to actual danger I don't suppose we should be exposed to any, but my poor Mary, & indeed all the children, it is grievous to think of the objections on their account. I should not mind in comparison, if Mary was to be shut up at Lambton for a year & ½ in solitude, but to think that the first society she is to meet with—& she has never had any of what you can call society—should be of this description we are likely to meet, & which we must partake of, it is really very, very hard.

The decision is not yet irrevocably taken, Lambton had a long interview with Ld. Melbourne yesterday, & has since had every moment filled up in speaking to other people—among them Henry[22] & Mr. Ellice, & to night I should think it must be settled as it seems they are very nearly agreed, & I have little hope that the negotiation will now break off. If we go we shall have to sail in April so as to be ready for the opening of the St. Lawrence in May—& I hope, my dearest Mary, that you will

soon come to town, & that at least we shall see as much of you
as possible till we go. We must also endeavour to look at the
bright side of the prospect & to hope that all will turn out for
the best. I will write again tomorrow; this day I have been so
tormented by great & little affairs (the servants plague me out
of my mind) that I have hardly known what I have said to you,
but my dearest dear Mary, cheer up a little & endeavour to think
a little better of the prospects of the case, tho' Heaven knows it
is painful enough to have such a separation to look forward to.
The weather is bitter & the house infinitely colder than I ever
felt it at Petersburgh. Give thousands of loves to Papa, Geor-
giana—a goodbye my dearest Mary.

Yr. most affect.
Louisa

MONDAY, 23 APRIL

We left Cleveland Row.²³ My sisters, Caroline & Georgiana, came to see us once again in the morning before we started. On stopping in the middle of the day for the children's dinner, we found Alice unwell & when she arrived at Portsmouth she was put to bed with a smart attack of Fever. We had rooms at the George Inn, where we assembled most of the party who were to embark with us, but we did not see them till next day. My brother Frederick,²⁴ Mr. Ponsonby, Mr. Ellice & Admiral Fleming²⁵ had come down to see us off, & dined with us. The weather in the evening was unfavorable, & there seemed little prospect of our being able to sail next morning.

TUESDAY, 24 APRIL

We were told in the morning that the wind had become fair, and that if we were on board the *Hastings* by one o'clock we should be able to go out by the Needles. Alice continued much in the same state, having been left in bed however until the last moment. She was then taken up & went down with me in a carriage to the Sally Port. Here we found the two Admirals, Sir Philip Durham²⁶ & Admiral Bouverie²⁷ & many other people waiting to see us embark. Sir P. Durham was very civil, & spoke of his Band

22

of Music which he had sent on board the Steamer that was to take us to the *Hastings* at Spithead, but this was not a moment that one could attend to such things. With all the agitating feelings of our departure, aggravated by seeing Alice ill & frightened, it was very distressing having to embark with so much noise & ceremony. That band in particular was very bewildering. Frederick carried Alice into the boat, on board the Steamer, & afterwards into the *Hastings*. (After being settled into the Cabin she got better, although she continued unwell for the first fortnight. As she continued, she enjoyed the voyage excessively & arrived at Quebec quite well.)

By the time every thing was embarked & the ship ready to weigh, it was found too late to go out by the Needles. We therefore were obliged to take leave of Frederick, Mr. Ponsonby & Mr. Ellice, who had come on board intending to accompany us as far as they could along the coast. As we went by St. Helens this was impossible.

The first night we did not advance much. The *Dee* Steamer & *Charybdis* were intended to accompany us, but the former got on shore in the afternoon, which delayed us some hours, & next morning, finding that neither of them kept up, we parted company. We had a good run out of the channel, but afterwards met with contrary winds & had a tedious passage. He was wearied with it, being impatient to arrive, but in health he was tolerably well.

Our party consisted of 22,[28] exclusive of the Officers belonging to the Ship. On the first day while we were still under the shelter of the land we all met at dinner, but the night was rough, & next day many were disabled & missing. [Lambton] & the children were not sea-sick, but I suffered a good deal at first, & Mrs. Ellice & her sister[29] were much worse. In time we got better & appeared again at the large dinner in the great cabin, when the weather was tolerably smooth. The arrangements for our accommodation were as comfortable as it was possible to make them. The After Cabin was divided into two sitting rooms, one for the Captain[30] & Gentlemen of the Suite, the other for ourselves. In both were Fire places & ours we constantly kept used. We had comfortable furniture—Sofa, Arm chairs &c. & a harp & Piano Forte, which were played a good deal when weather permitted. Mrs. Ellice, too, often sang. No one came into this cabin without invitation, excepting her & her sister, but when the weather was tolerably fine we stayed most of the morning on deck. The girls walked a great deal & Mary often drew. It was very cold at times but this they did not mind. He, also, was out a great deal, though part of the day he usually employed on business in his cabin. He had a separate cabin below, but remained chiefly upstairs on account of the cold.

THURSDAY, 3 MAY
A whale was seen spouting in the wake of the ship.

FRIDAY, 4 MAY
The weather was very fine & we remained on deck till near 7 o'clock, but in the evening the wind began to blow hard from the SW & in the course of the night increased to a heavy gale which continued till the afternoon of the next day. We had dreadful confusion in the cabins, the furniture breaking loose in all directions. George[31] was nearly knocked out of his cot & was carried out from amidst the fragments of his dressing things & the water which had washed in at the Port. The maids were also in great trouble. The sea washed in upon them & one of them was washed out of her bed. He went on deck in the night, & remained there a great deal during the continuance of the Storm. At one time the Quarter Deck guns were rolling under water. The Ship was made snug with close-reefed topsails & storm jib & staysail. Towards the afternoon the wind became more moderate & by degrees, then & the next day, things were put in order again. He did every thing that was possible for our comfort when the ship was rolling so heavily that it was scarcely possible to stand. I remained for some time in his writing cabin with Alice on my lap.

WEDNESDAY, 9 MAY
[It] was a fine day but there was a dead calm in the afternoon.

24

A boat was lowered, & He & the Children were rowed round the Ship. The moon at night was beautiful. The next three days we had warm weather, but with a good deal of rain.

H.M.S. Hastings, At Sea
10 May

My dearest Mary,
We have now been above a fortnight at sea, and though I have often had it in my thoughts to begin writing to you, I have never felt sufficiently reconciled to the Ship to make the attempt. Now however, I think I am at last getting more used to it, & as the day is fine & the motion trifling, the beginning shall be made.

We embarked, as you know, on Tuesday April the 24th, but as we were delayed by the Steamers, we can hardly say we made a start till the next morning when we parted company with them, & soon after with the Charybdis. *We got very prosperously out of the channel, & had in general favorable winds till the 4th having made above 700 miles. After that the wind began to blow from the SW & for the best part of one night & day we had a very heavy gale making sad confusion & disturbance in the cabins. I wish all the inconvenience could have been endured by the provoking people who had been wishing for a storm, but I fear it fell most heavily upon the minority. However all comes to an end, good or bad & we very soon got to rights again, but it was provoking at the end of 3 days to find ourselves 40 miles further back than we were before the change. We have had a great deal of motion even since the wind abated, and what there was of it, being contrary, were not able to make our course, I think, till yesterday & then we had a calm all the afternoon. However, the weather was so fine, and the sea so beautiful that I think no one grumbled at the little delay, & this morning I am in hopes we are going right. You will conclude by my not having mentioned it sooner that we are all very well & so we are. L had one bad attack in his head but since that he has been looking a good deal better than he had done for some time. Alice was not very well at first, having a cold and being sea-sick but within the last few days she looks herself again. Emily was rather sick and squeamish at first, but neither Mary or George have had half an hours discomfort. As for me, I was very sick for some days & very uncomfortable for a long time. I could not eat neither breakfast or dinner for at least 10 days, only swallowing now and then, when I could, some mulled Port or some hot mutton broth. However as there are few toils without some good belonging to them, there has been this advantage in the general sickness of the Ladies—for Mrs. Ellice & Miss Balfour were still worse —that we have been emancipated from the long, hot dinner of the whole company. Mrs. E. & Miss B. still, I believe, eat nothing but sweetmeats, the last things I would touch, at odd times, & I, now that I can eat, have my dinner with the children, staying not a moment longer than I like, & my breakfast in my own cabin while I dress. We sit most of the morning on deck. Mary & Mrs. E. draw a great deal & in the evening we have a fire in our sitting cabin which looks very snug & into which none of the suite have the privilege of entering—in short our arrangements are all very comfortable, as much so as it is possible they should be at Sea, but at the best I still infinitely prefer some discomfort on dry land. And now, my dearest Mary, having done pretty well I think in writing a whole sheet for the first time, I shall cease for the present. I was very, very sorry that any letters were sent from the ship, without one from me, but I was not told in time & tho' I wrote a line instantly the boat was just going off when it was sent.*

SUNDAY, 13 MAY

There was a very sudden change to great cold, a difference of nearly 20 degrees having taken place in the Thermometer in the course of one night. We were now on the Banks of Newfoundland & remained there for some days, with changeable winds & very disagreeable weather.

MONDAY, 14 MAY

When we were on the Great Bank we lay to for fishing. Several fine Cod were taken, & more were hooked, but lost by the impatience of those who pulled the lines to raise them up. The sea was very clear, & it was a curious sight to see these immense creatures dragged up the side of the Ship. We met with some fishing boats. The weather continued very cold all the time we were near the banks, & we had a great deal of drizzling fog & contrary wind.

15*May*

We are now on the great bank of Newfoundland & stopped yesterday for an hour or two to fish, very successfully, as several large cod were taken to the great joy, I believe, of the Commander on board. We had been some days getting on almost without motion & yesterday in consequence were brought to dine in the large cabin, but I don't know whether we must hope for the continuance of such delightful quiet. I trust we are not threatened with a gale, but we are getting into a little roll. The weather too has been dreadfully cold for the last day or two, one evening after a sort of day we were almost complaining of the heat, but on getting up next morning we found the thermometer had fallen above 20 degrees & we were perished with cold. We are to hope for fine weather when we are clear of the banks, but all this morning it has been raining & the children have not been able to get on deck. However we ought not to complain as we can have a good fire in our sitting cabin. It is wonderful, considering that we have now been on board 3 weeks, how little we have seen of the suite, some of them indeed I have scarcely spoken to & one of the number I fear is my cousin W. Ponsonby, but he appears little on deck & is I imagine, extremely shy. The only person who has got a word out of him is Mrs. Ellice, but he has told her he does not like the sea, so I hope that we shall get on better on shore. By the bye I must tell you that Dr. Quire's powders have had a most signal triumph. There were on board two absolute martyrs to sea-sickness, Mr. A. Buller & Mrs. Ellice's maid; the former had been ill for above a fortnight but was at last quite restored by taking them, in consequence of which, they were administered to the maid & were equally successful with her. I am not an advocate for homeopathy, but I must bear witness to {these results.}

THURSDAY, 17 MAY

In the Evening Mr. Turton,[32] Mr. Buller[33] &c. with His assistance got up a trial scene in the dining cabin. I do not remember the particulars of it, but we all laughed a great deal. No one could promote a little fun like him. He entered into it & laughed so heartily!

SATURDAY, 19 MAY

The deck & rigging were covered with ice in the morning. It was supposed we were near Icebergs altho' we saw none. The day was fine but bitterly cold.

SUNDAY, 20 MAY

About 4 in the afternoon we came in sight of Cape Scatari.

TUESDAY, 22 MAY

In the afternoon we were near Anticosti.

New Anticosti
May 22

My dearest Mary,
We came in sight of land (Cape Scatari) the day before yesterday & had the wind continued as it was on that day we should now have been in the river, perhaps under convoy of the steamers which we hope are looking out for us, but such good fortune was not to be ours. Yesterday there was a strong breeez against us & tho' it is now moderated & less unfavorable we are not yet keeping our course & have made but 20 miles in the last 24 hours. The last two or three days have been bright & clear, but before that we had very bad weather & it has been, & still is, bitterly cold. We make our sitting cabin warm & comfortable, but it requires courage to go out of it into the sleeping cabins. Mary has got a little cough, but I trust it will not be much if we can only just get into a little warmer weather, though I am rather afraid too it may not be very good even when we get up the river. The land we saw yesterday had snow on it &, I forgot to tell you, the decks & the rigging were covered with ice two or three morn-

28

ings. Lambton keeps pretty well considering, but this cold is very trying to him & makes me angry with the people in London who were in such a hurry to send him off because they could not face the observations of the H. of Commons. They say we should have had—as it turned out—a quicker passage if we had steered for the Bermudas, but it was not to be fore seen at this time of year that we should have had so much westerly wind.

WEDNESDAY, 23 MAY
A pilot came on board (a French Canadian) & we received News-papers from Quebec, in which we found among other things that the House of Assembly[34] had been taken for us by Col. Couper.[35] We also met a homeward bound Ship by which we sent letters.

THURSDAY, 24 MAY
A fine day but little wind. In celebration of the Queen's birthday there was a parade & salute at 12 o'clock. He gave a dinner in the Gun room to the Officers of the Ship & the Suite. The children were also present. There were toasts & speeches after dinner, the company all appearing highly pleased & in great spirits. He knew well how to carry off this sort of thing, & Capt. Locke with all his shyness seemed as happy as the rest. In the evening the Officers got up a ball on the Quarter Deck which was prettily arranged with Flags, & the dancing was very gay.

May 24
We got on famously the day before yesterday when I last wrote —going 10 knots with a very fair breeze—& were in sight of Anticosti in the afternoon, but the wind changed early next morng. and was strong against us all day, giving us more motion than we expected to have had. Now we are arrived in the narrow seas. We met yesterday morng. a homeward bound ship, & I had just time to write you a few lines saying we were all well. I would not send this letter because I thought it would go more surely by the packet after we arrive, but I was rather inclined last night to regret not having done so, for a pilot came on board who dis-couraged us exceptionally in our hopes of a change of wind &

told us we might still be kept a long time before we could get up.
However I am happy to say he is at least partly wrong, for we
are now going right, & when we get a little further I trust we
may meet Steamers which may be of use to us. We had also
yesterday Newspapers from Quebec by which we learned that
the Malabar *had arrived in 20 days, but we were much disap-*
pointed to find that the 71st[36] had gone on to Montreal. We had
been rejoicing so much in the idea of finding Charles & Mrs.
Charles.[37] This being the Queen's birthday we are to have a large
dinner with all the Officers of the Ship, which including our own
party & children will amount to 56 people. They had talked of
having it under canvas on the poop, but I am happy to say this
project is given up, & that they have found room for it in the
Gun room. The weather is much too cold for those airy proceed-
ings. We are also to have a play to morrow or some night while
we are on the river. The getting up of this has been a great occu-
pation & amusement to the gentlemen & Officers & I suppose
will make us laugh one way or another.

SATURDAY, 26 MAY

We had now entered the St. Lawrence, but were obliged to lay
to for some time in the morning on account of a thick fog, &
though we were able to proceed afterwards, the weather was
rough & disagreeable & continued all day so hazy that little
could be seen. We passed the *Edinburgh*, 74, at anchor near the
Brandy Pots, waiting for a fair wind to continue her voyage
home. About 8 o'clock in the Evening we anchored 36 miles from
Quebec.

This evening were represented some Theatricals which had
been in preparation during a great part of the voyage, altho' from
the want of smooth weather there had hitherto been no opportunity of performing them. This last night, however, it was
determined they should take place, & as soon as every thing was
in readiness (which was not till 10 o'clock) we were called upon
to witness the performance of *The Critic* & *Tom Thumb* by the
Gentlemen & Officers of the Ship. Mr. Buller, Mr. Turton &
Mr. Bouverie[38] acted very well, & we laughed very much. It was

one in the morning before all was concluded.

We anchored at 4 in the morning & were early on deck to behold
the banks of the St. Lawrence. The size of the River is magnificent but we perceived at first no very striking feature in the
banks. As we advanced, however, the outline of the hills on the
right became more bold, & on approaching Quebec it is very fine.
We were also struck with a look of bareness in the country, & the
appearance of the wood, in which fir trees alone caught our view,
seemed meagre & poor. This, however, was not the case later in
the year,[39] when the forest trees were in leaf & diversified the
formality of the others. At this time there was scarcely any commencement of vegetation, & remains of snow were to be seen in
many places along the banks. The weather was fine tho' cold &
the wind fair & we advanced rapidly, passing the Island of
Orleans, & the falls of Montmorenci, till at last we came in sight
of Quebec, where we anchored about one o'clock, below the citadel, near the Ships of War which had already arrived & which
added greatly to the beauty of the scene. If we had been inclined
to feel disappointment on the first part of our passage up the St.
Lawrence, our expectations were now fulfilled to the utmost.
The situation of the town is magnificent. The rock on which it is
built advances upon the river, which on one side forms a large
basin into which runs the river St. Charles, while on the other,
looking up the stream as it approaches from Montreal, the scenery is lovely & beautiful to the greatest degree. The banks
which on the right are very steep, are clothed with wood & scattered with Villas. Below, a succession of coves for many miles are
filled with rafts of timber, & enlivened by the Shipping employed
in receiving their cargoes.

There is a succession of small villages & single houses along
the banks of the St. Lawrence, beginning far below Quebec &
continuing with little interruption to Montreal, & again above,
giving the appearance of a long line of Street. Around Quebec
the country is dotted with white houses which look like a vast
collection of tents. Near the churches, of which there are a great

number, there is always one, & sometimes two, small houses. In these are deposited the bodies of those who die in the winter & who are not buried in the Church Yards until the breaking up of the frost.

May 29

I have been on the watch, my dearest Mary, for an opportunity to send my letter but none has yet offered. The weather was so bad yesterday that Lambton's landing was deferred till to day at 2 o'clock. We shall go on shore to see it, but return to sleep on board, & tomorrow we go to stay, & dine with Sir John Colborne. This is convenient enough to the servants, but I am rather disturbed about dress, for there has been no possibility of looking at any thing on board ship, & I fear I shall find nothing but what is very homely or very fine & there is also a rumour that a very essential box is left behind.

You will be glad to hear that the account of the Assembly House is very favorable. They say the rooms are very good, they have been new painted or cleaned & the view is beautiful. There is also some sort of a garden at the Chateau[10] & must be a hot house, for they brought me a nosegay of Rose Geranium which was welcomed with positive joy. In short, I am agreeably surprised in the idea that we shall be comfortable as far as house & lodging are concerned. By the bye, this puts me in mind that I have been very ungrateful in not telling you before how comfortable we have been made in the ship. Nothing could answer better than all the arrangements that were made about the cabins & as far as Captain Locke it is impossible that any one should have been more kind or more anxious to do every thing that could be agreeable to us in every way. The Commander also, Captain Worth,[11] became a great favourite with the children, who indeed made friends with all the Officers of the Ship.

I have had much more leisure for writing than I had expected owing to our remaining these two days on board, but still I have not attempted letters to any of my Sisters or brothers except Mary[12] who I suppose to be abroad. I had many little letters to write, & I thought it better to tell you all I could than to divide

what I had to say among several as you are so many together—
depending upon you giving them an account of us—but I hope
you will tell them that I think of each & shall write to them by
degrees. Will you also give my best love to Uncle Harry & Ldy.
Grey[13] *& tell the latter I shall write to her after I think you have*
left London. Mary also means to tell her how useful she has
found the Drawing apparatus she gave her.

TUESDAY, 29 MAY

He made his public entry accompanied by Sir John Colborne[14]
who, with his Staff, received him at the Wharf. They proceeded
on horseback (all in Uniform) to the old Chateau & as we followed in an open carriage up the steep streets of the town, crowds
of people lining the way on each side, the effect of the procession
was very striking. At the Chateau He took the Oaths, & afterwards returned to the *Hastings*, which we did not finally leave
till next day. His reception was considered most favorable by all
who were acquainted with the Colony. To those accustomed to
public demonstrations in England, the cheering might have
seemed faint, but there was great appearance of respect.

May 31

My dearest Mary,
The Edinburgh *sails to morrow & will take our letters which I*
hope will reach you quickly, but in general I believe we shall
write by the New York Packets. I send you some Newspapers
with the accounts of Lambton's landing so I have only to add
that hitherto every thing seems to go in the most promising man-
ner. L is delighted with the interviews he has had with Sir J.
Colborne. He says nothing could be more satisfactory & Sir
John is most sanguine as to the possibility of a favorable termina-
tion to all the difficulties of the affair.

We landed yesterday to stay. We are tolerably off in the Inn[15]
& shall be delightfully lodged in the Assembly house. We have
this morning been distributing all the rooms & as soon as the
Furniture is unpacked, which I hope will be in a very few days,
we shall remove there. The horses are all arrived safe & Lamb-

ton & the children are just going to ride.

Thousands of loves again & again & good bye my dearest Mary. We are all quite well but dying to hear from you.

Yr. most affect.

Louisa

The Hastings will go back next week. I hope to find some Indian things to send by it.

FRIDAY, 1 JUNE

We remained the month of June at Quebec, being lodged after the first fortnight in the House of Assembly which had been hastily fitted up for our reception. During this time he was generally well in health & in good spirits, pleased with the prospect of success which seemed to attend his enterprise. The general expectation that had awaited his arrival, the hopes that it inspired of more decided & efficient measures for the settlement of the Country, & the favorable impression which he produced personally upon all who approached him, seemed to justify these anticipations. His communications with Sir John Colborne were of the most friendly nature, & during the whole time of his stay the utmost cordiality prevailed between them. Indeed nothing could exceed the frankness & consideration for the feelings of others which invariably marked his conduct at all times in his behaviour towards those with whom he was connected in the public service. From the moment of his arrival he devoted himself unremittingly to business & the morning hours were so completely occupied that he could scarcely ever find leisure for the air & exercise which were so necessary to his health. When he could, he drove or went out with me & the children in the afternoon, but he was constantly interrupted. We were all very anxious that he should make it a rule never to see any one after a certain hour, but we could not obtain it. The morning hours being thus employed in serious business, there was little relaxation in those of the evening, for he had every day a large dinner. The principal persons of the place were all invited in succession, besides the Officers of the Army & Navy, & although two days in the week were especially set apart for company, there were so

34

many people to see, & the suite was so numerous, that it was little more than a trifling difference in numbers. We were never fewer than 3 or 4 & twenty, & on the great days 40 or more.

Quebec
June 2nd

My dearest Mary,
The Edinburgh *has not been able to get away on account of the East Wind which by the bye I must tell you is as disagreeable here as in other parts of the world. I suspect too the weather is not often very pleasant, probably the heat consists in a very broiling sun, & the refreshing breeze they talk of is most likely a cold wind in the shade & in the evg.—in short I should imagine it is a disagreeable place to live in, tho' from the great abuse I had heard at first, I was inclined to be more favorable for the first day or two.*

Lambton seems very well satisfied with all that is going on here, but this American business of the Steamer [16] *is too vexatious —you will of course see the whole account of it.*

Our house is getting on & as it is airy & spacious it will be a great pleasure to remove into it, & we shall submit with patience to a little want of Furniture. The Housekeeper is very useful, but the servants in general are great plagues, & dreadfully hard to please & unreasonable. The blunders that have been made too, are inconceivable, quantities of things which we could have spared for months have been brought, & others most essential left behind. I have not a cap or a coiffure for the evg. except the faded half cap I wore for the last week in London—not even a ribbon to trim one, & at last I am obliged to hunt out, & buy things here to make up. However I don't believe it will very much signify except for our own people, what we have, & I am determined to resist finery every day, tho' we are so many at dinner without strangers that it looks as if one ought to be smart. We have hitherto continued to dine in the Inn, but to day we are to go to Ld. Gosford's [17] *dining room in the remains of the Castle. They say there never was such a place seen as the room he slept in, in the same building.*

Sunday Morng. 3rd.

*The wind is, I believe, fair & I must make up my letter before
Church. I send a bottle belonging to my dressing box as a pattern
for one I wish to have made to replace it, as you will see it is
broken, tho' not sufficiently so to prevent its serving as a measure.
The neck of it had been made much too thin. I have no shop
where I wish it to be done so that I leave it to you & the agent
at the Colonial Office will forward it.*

*Dining at the Castle yesterday was far better than at the Inn.
There are two very good rooms which will do excellently for
balls without disturbing us in our own house, when it is necessary
to have them.*

*Thousands of loves from Lambton & the children to all.
Charles is sent for here & we expect him in a day or two. Good
bye my dearest Mary.*

Yr. most affect.
Louisa

TUESDAY, 5 JUNE

Once only, a day or two after our arrival, we were quite a small
party. Charles & Caroline, who had arrived in the morning from
Montreal, were with us, but nearly the whole suite dined on
board the *Hastings*. (He had a Levee [this] morning). The dinners were at the Chateau till the dining room was ready at the
House of Assembly, which was not for some time after we went
to live there. These dinners were very fatiguing. They were very
long & in the hot weather (of which we had a great deal, altho'
during this month it was changeable) very oppressive. Col.
Couper managed the invitations & we sometimes thought him
quite cruel in not allowing us more rest, but so little were we ever
in private that I never saw Him dine out of Uniform from the
day we landed till that on which we reembarked to return home.
I found the civilities to the ladies very toilsome. It was not easy
to find topics of conversation, they were in general shy & ill at
ease, but it was necessary to be very exact in attention to all in
order to avoid giving offence. Mary, & Caroline Grey, Mrs.
Ellice & her sister, did their best to assist me, & Caroline was of

36

great use in sitting by him at dinner as he had thereby only one strange Lady next to him to attend to in particular. We found music a recourse in the Evg. Not that it often happened there was any one who seemed to care about it, but it made something to do, & helped conversation.

The girls & I found this life very irksome at first, & I fear we complained of it more than we should have done. Habit reconciled us to it in some degree, or at least rendered it more easy, & at least we had always the whole morning to ourselves. We never made visits or went out anywhere, the only exceptions which occurred were a dinner the day of our landing at Sir J. Colborne's, & a Ball on board the *Hastings* which was given by the Captain & Officers before their return to England. We had also a party with the same Officers round the Island of Orleans & the Falls of Montmorenci, in a Steamer on board of which we dined, & another to the Chaudière Falls. On the latter occasion business prevented his accompanying us, but not unluckily, as it turned out, for we were overtaken by a violent shower of rain, & obliged to go some way on the rough carioles of the country, besides getting wet. The Falls of Montmorenci are very fine from their great height, but gain little from the surrounding landscape. They are best seen from the River on approaching Quebec. The Chaudière Falls are more beautiful in point of scenery, particularly at the beginning of the summer when the melting of the snow has afforded a large supply of water. Late in the season they are nearly dry, as is the case with most of the falls in the country around Quebec.

June 5

My dearest Mary,
We are at last lodged in the H. of Assembly but we still go backwards & forwards to the Castle—even the children—to dinner & have got a great deal to do to be settled. We are now suffering from heat. I don't know that one should have found it too much if it had not exactly increased one's fatigue in flitting, or if we had plenty of blinds, but they are not yet ready & this house tho' airy, is very broiling. There is a large room, a library, which will

soon be very comfortable.

I send you a few specimens of the Indian Bark Work. I think the Porcupine quills like Mrs. Cokeby's old boxes are prettier, but they are chiefly made at Halifax, & we have not yet found any nice ones. The two flat pieces for Papa I thought might be useful to put his cup upon. We are to have another expedition to morrow with the Hastings people to the Chaudière falls. It is a little bit of a plague as I dread Lambton's being knocked up with the trips of every kind, but they are bent upon it, & Capt. Lock is so kind & good natured that one is anxious to please him. He has promised, by the bye, to call upon you, & give you the last account of us, & I think you will be glad to see him, but you must remember that he is the shyest man that ever was. I will add a few lines to my letter at the last moment. I am quite ashamed of sending one so full of blunders but the constant interruptions & the flitting have bothered my head. Lambton was very unwell with a feverish attack for two days, but is now better, & we are all well. Dr. Doratt[48] has been very seriously, even dangerously, ill, but he came out again to day for the first time. I think this climate requires a little care, the changes are so very sudden. I cannot imagine how England has got its reputation for inconstancy of weather. It seems to me that changeable as it may be, it is much less so than most others.

June 13th

I am going to put up my letter for the Hastings which is expected to sail to morrow early, but I shall write again on the 15th by the Messenger to New York & that letter may probably reach you first.

We received the letters by the Medea yesterday, but the Colonial Office Despatches are not yet arrived. Thousands & thousands of loves to Papa & all.

Yr. most affect.
Louisa

WEDNESDAY, 13 JUNE   49

We had a Drawing Room in the Evg. which was very fully attended. I found [it] a formidable busines, but many of our party were, I believe, much amused. The weather was excessively hot.

Monday June 14
My dearest Mary,

I do not know when the Hastings *will sail as the Admiral*[50] 50 *arrived last night & she will now await his orders, so that I send my letter to morrow by New York.*

Lambton has been very much in want of the Admiral who has been long expected, & tho' I trust He has had the means of doing all that was necessary, I am very glad he has come to assist him. Every one tells me that all things go on in the Province as one could wish, but the Pirates and the Frontiers[51] 51 *are a plague, & the turmoil in which we have hitherto lived I think very tiresome. In short I give many a sigh to home on many accounts.*

The Medea *brought me your letters of the 8th & 11th of May, but those you refer to of an earlier date are not yet arrived. I believe the* Post *to New York is much the quickest way of hearing, & tho' I must not interfere with the general orders for sending our letters thro' the Col. Off.,*[52] 52 *I should be very glad if you would write to me in that way, under cover, of course, to Lambton. There are regular Packets from Liverpool 4 times a month & they tell me during the summer they are very certain. I cannot thank you enough for your letters or tell you how happy I was to hear. By the bye the* Madeira *Passenger's News may not have been false, we were a long way South of our course, & some of our guns were under water on the morning of the gale. We had not a quick passage, but as out of the 35 days we were at sea, we had 20 on which the wind was not favorable, we ought perhaps to think ourselves lucky that it was not slower.*

The Drawing Room took place last night, & I am happy it is over tho' it was much more easily got through than I expected. There were about 200 ladies, every one that ought to come, & a much larger number of gentlemen but they went by so very

39

quickly that it looked a very short time, & I was neither hotter or more tired at the end than I was before it began. The ladies had all done their best in dressing, & were smarter than I expected, but seemed in a great fright. That they are also when they come to dinner, particularly with Lambton, tho' he does all he can to put them at their ease. I cannot help telling you that the one he took out to dinner the other day, who had been given to him as the highest person present, eat Jelly *with her knife!*

This is a beautiful place to see for a day, & we shall be glad to have been to Niagara, but it does give me a pang when I hear of other girls in England, to think that my dear Mary is passing her time in society like this. If it ends with this year well & good, but I dislike the thought of remaining so much on every account, that I shall not be able to trust to our going so soon till I see the preparations actually begun. George has not been quite well this day or two, the sudden change & heat of the weather have I think affected him, but I trust that he will soon be right again. He was not the better for another expedition we had with the Hastings *people the day before yesterday, to the Chaudière falls, which I think are much prettier than Montmorenci, but after landing from the Steamer we had to go 2 or 3 miles in the carioles of the country, & we were caught in a heavy rain & had to {come} back in a hurry, we were nearly jolted to pieces. Lambton had been kept at home by business, & as it turned out I was very glad. The heat has been very overpowering for the last few days. I don't know that I should have found it so if I had been able to sit still in a cool room till evg., but this I could not do & I have, besides, been tormented by bugs at night, so that I have scarcely had a good sleep since I came to this house. In general I am not a victim to those creatures, tho' I am dreadfully disturbed by the notion of them, but this time they have attacked me more than the children. Every bit of furniture we have is new, but they crawl out of the floors, & it seems one cannot get into a house any where out of England without having some nuisance of this kind to encounter. However I trust we shall soon overcome these difficulties. The kitchen & eating at the Chateau is still a plague —worse for the servants than for us—but we are making our rooms very comfortable.*

Pray give my best love to Papa & all. Excepting George's little indisposition we are all quite well. Good bye my dearest Mary.

Yr. most affect.
Louisa

Saty. 16 *June*

My dearest Mary,
Your first letter of the 2nd & 6th of May arrived this morng. & I have just an opportunity of telling you how welcome it was in spite of it being an older date than those I had received before. I am delighted you put Eliza into Cleveland Row, but I am not surprised you had difficulty with the Housekeeper, as she had very strict orders in consequence of what had happened about Ldy. Dartmouth not to let any one in, without hearing from us. I cannot say how pleased I am that you are fond of the pictures of the children. I am delighted that I left them with you. I am very sorry for the attacks on Mr. Turton, but happily they have done no mischief here. All parties agree on the absolute necessity of standing by him now, & Lambton says the use he has been of to him in the legal business is incalculable. It is a thousand pities there is this blot in his former character, for now he seems to be unexceptionable, & when one sees him it is really difficult to believe there ever could have been any thing wrong. He is extremely gentleman-like, quiet, & kind in his manner; that he is exactly the person one should choose to rely on as a friend. I cannot understand it in the least.

I don't understand, my dearest Mary, what difficulty there can be about the postage. Surely the Govr. may receive what letters he pleases, & you need not think of a single sheet. I hope I am under no mistake in this matter for depending upon our letters going in a bag. I have sent you heaps of trash which I am sure was not worth paying for. I am doing so now, but I know a messenger takes a bag this evening to New York & from there I believe it will be forwarded in the same way by the consul.

George is quite well again but we must be careful now in not

*allowing him or any of the children, to go out in the heat of the
day.*

Thousands & thousands of loves.

Yr. most affect.

Louisa

*Quebec
June 27th*

My dearest Mary,

The Hercules *will not sail till to morrow night or the following
morning, but as I may not have much time to spare in the course
of to morrow, I will begin my letter to day. I have however little
to tell you since I wrote last. Lambton has been very busy & very
anxious about the affair of the prisoners,*[53] *but he is well satisfied
at the line of conduct which their course has enabled him to
pursue, & I trust all will go well. The newspapers, I conclude,
will give you all details & I will only add that it will be very
gratifying if Lambton's measures succeed, as every one agrees
that it was a hard case the decision of this matter should have
been left to him on his arrival. Perhaps it could scarcely have
been helped, but at any rate it is most satisfactory that Sir J.
Colborne now agrees with him entirely & is most cordial.*

*I rather dread the Ball to morrow night, but if it is only fine
enough to go out into the garden, it will be a great thing for the
crowd & as we have had our 3 cold & rainy days it is likely that
the weather will now be favorable—it will also be a great advantage if it does not became hotter than it is at present. We shall
have heat again I dare say, but I hope the excess will not be felt
till after this day. The evening itself will of course be tiresome,
but I must own that it is a comfort that none of the fuss preceding
it falls upon us. Col. Couper manages the invitations & the
preparations, & I have nothing to do but to be dressed ready to
receive the company. We are all delighted to have kept Charles
& Caroline to help us. He was very impatient to get back to his
regiment but as Lambton wanted him on business he was obliged
to stay. They will also accompany us on our tour.*

The Catholic Bishop of Upper Canada, a Macdonald of Glen-

garry,[54] dined here yesterday. He speaks broad Scotch, but seems
perfectly acquainted with all that is going on in England. He
told me he first remembered seeing Papa in '92 & he had heard
him speak in the H. of Commons on some occasion when Mr.
Fox, Mr. Pitt, Mr. Sheridan, Mr. Tierney—had also spoken,
but that he thought none of them equalled Papa in delivery. He
said too that when he was young he was the most elegant man he
ever saw in his life. Sir. J. Macdonald[55] who commands the garri-
son, is of his clan & he is going to take him up to the district of
Glengarry above Montreal to see his Countrymen who are settled there. Ldy. Catherine Harcourt[56] is arrived with some other
ladies of the Guards. They have had a much more fatiguing
expedition with the land journey from New York than if they
had come here directly, but I do not think Lady C. looks worse
than she did in London. She dined here the other day. Ldy. M.
Hope was to have done so also but was too unwell. We were
yesterday on board the Cornwallis with the Admiral & afterwards visited the Malabar & the Inconstant. On leaving the
latter Lambton had the most frightful fall, he slipped & fell
head foremost down the accomodation ladder & if Sir C. Paget,
with wonderful strength & presence of mind had not stretched
out his hand to break his fall, he would have pitched with his
head upon an Iron knob which might have fractured his skull.

Quebec
June 28th

My dearest Mary,
I cannot say how distressed I am to hear of the dreadful anxiety
which you have all had to go through about dear little Mary
Barrington.[57] I trust it has been long over, & that by this time she
is almost as well as ever, but I shall be very anxious to hear again,
& it is vexatious to think how long we shall be without doing so
as the Gt. Western brought the last news in 14 days to New York
& no other ship is likely to make the voyage in double the time.
It is impossible to say how much I pity Caroline, & indeed all of
you for what you must have endured. I do hope that I shall hear
that you are none of you the worse for it, & that Georgiana has

neither caught the disorder or suffered from fatigue, but it is terrible to have the Atlantic between us & when I hear of afflictions, even those in which I am not interested, I cannot help feeling uncomfortable for all those I love. I think however I may feel confident about little Mary—once a child of that age begins to rally, after a violent attack of that sort, I think it generally recovers, & with all my heart I trust it is the case with her.

I have now received all your letters up to the 31st of May, those of the 22nd having arrived this morning. I was glad to hear of your having received news of us on our way, but my anger was brought back again in full force, it was too hard that you were the only person without a letter, & I cannot forgive the boat's not having been allowed to wait one moment for my poor note. I had got up the moment I was told, but it was all owing to my good nature in going to ask Lambton if he wanted to send any thing, which lost the one or two minutes by which I was too late. You will, of course, hear from Charles who returned from his journey yesterday, looking very sunburnt & perhaps a little thinner, but well. His mission seems to have had great effect,[58] *indeed the affairs of the Province seem to go on in a way which surpasses all expectations, but as to the place & the way of life, the less that is said about that the better. The country is beautiful, but what good does that do when the roads are impassable. I enjoy looking out of the window at the beautiful view, but that is all. Then the heat has been* overpowering *& the dreadful dinners & the dreadful ladies in the midst of it, really with every wish to make the best of things, I have just felt wearied in mind & body to a degree that I cannot describe. We have a cool day at last, thank heaven, & we are going in a week on a tour to the Upper Province which will interrupt the dinners, & give us an opportunity of seeing all the fine scenery of the country, but we are to have a ball & great doings for the Coronation on the 20th. I am sorry to say Caroline will be gone, as Charles must return to his regiment on Monday, but they will both, I believe, accompany us on our tour.*

We are at last quite in the Assembly House, having dined here for the first time yesterday. This will make us more comfortable

44

*& if the weather continues at its present temperature, & I get
rid of the creatures which still infest my room—the only one in
the house so plagued—I shall be in better humour. As it is I
rather reproach myself with having grumbled to you as I have
done, for after all we have the morning to ourselves & a delightful sitting room to live in. Capt. Lock, who I am sure will go to
see you as soon as he arrives, will give you an account of it, &
also tell you that we are all well. I do not say that Lambton has
not occasionally a little attack, but I am astonished, considering
all things, to see him as well as he is. Thousands of loves to all &
pray say to Caroline how much I think of her & feel for her. I
shall have an opportunity of writing again in two days by another
ship. Good bye my dearest Mary,*

*Yr. most affect.
Louisa*

Pray make my kind congratulations to John & Ldy. J. E.[59] 59

THURSDAY, 28 JUNE

The Coronation Day. We went before 11 o'clock to the plains of
Abraham where there was a Review of the Guards, Salutes from
the Citadel & the Ships, & a *Feu de Joie* from the Troops on the
Ground. He was there on horseback. George was with him but
his poney, not being used to firing, reared at [the] noise & he was
taken off. As we returned it began to rain & heavy showers continued to fall almost with[out] interruption for the remainder of
the Afternoon & Evening. We had a Ball at the Chateau &
preparations had been made for illuminating the garden, but the
rain rendered them useless. There were Rockets from the Citadel
& Fireworks were attempted on board the Ships, of course with
little effect, altho' such as they were we were told they were
much admired. The Ball was very crowded, but it was not
thought necessary that we should stay it out, & we returned home
soon after one in the morning.

On this day were published the Act of Amnesty, with the
famous Ordinances relating to the Prisoners[60] 60 measures requiring great courage & decision & involving, as it afterwards proved,

too fatal a responsibility, but completely answering the objects they were intended to effect in the country.

He wrote on this day a letter of Congratulation to the Queen, rejoicing that he had been enabled to grant an Act of Amnesty & Grace in her name, considering it the best tribute he could offer her on that memorable day.

The penal measures (& they were merciful) were done in his own name. This wise & generous conduct it was, which met with so unworthy a return. The policy which was acquiesced in, & applauded by the continent of America, could meet with no support among his own friends or from his miserable Employers in the Govt. at home—approving as they did, in private, most entirely, of what he had done, they yet abandoned him without a struggle in the H. of Lords to the attacks of a faction consisting of their own worst enemies & thus overthrew at once every plan in which he was engaged (& hitherto with the fairest prospects of success) for the advantage & improvement of a great country, at the same time sealing the fate of one for whom they professed public & private Friendship.

Lord John Russell,[61] alone among the Ministers, deserves some exemption to this censure. But this is Anticipation, & does not belong to the present moment, the day of of the Coronation on which the Ordinances were published at Quebec.

I should have mentioned that on the Anniversary of Waterloo (June 18th) he gave a dinner to Sir John Colborne & all the Officers (of whom there were several at Quebec) who had been present at that occasion, there was a large party & after dinner he gave their healths with speeches, which were gratifying to them.

I had also forgot a visit to the Convent of Ursuline Nuns[62] on Monday 25th. They had arranged a kind of Theatrical reception & Welcome for Him, presented an Address, garlands of Flowers &c. It was difficult to refrain from laughing at some of these ceremonies, but it was all done to shew their good will, and was thought a good deal of amongst the French Canadians. We always found the ladies seemed pleased when we spoke of our visit or shewed the ornamental address.

Sir Charles Paget, the Admiral of the Station, had arrived at

Quebec June 23rd., & from that time till he left the country, lived almost constantly with us. Nothing could exceed his kindness, both in public & private, & He always met with the most cordial cooperation & support from him in every way.

He visited him (with us) on board the *Cornwallis*, his Flag Ship, on the 26th, & afterwards went with him to see the *Malabar* & *Inconstant*. On leaving the latter to get into the boat, He slipped down the accommodation ladder, & had not the Admiral with great strength & presence of mind caught & broken his fall, the consequences might have been most serious. His head nearly hit against a strong Iron stancheon at the foot of the ladder. His hat was knocked off but he was not hurt in any way.

Genl. Clitherow,[63] the General commanding at Montreal, had visited him early & Sir John Harvey,[64] the Govr. of New Brunswick, arrived on the 29th & remained till the day we set out for Montreal.

June 29

My dearest Mary,
The Coronation rejoicings are happily over & as every one knows we did our best, it is all well, but the weather completely spoiled the evening. It just held up for the review in the morning which was very pretty but it then came on to rain & we had heavy showers during the rest of the day & the evening which spoilt all the illuminations & prevented our going into the garden. The ball was exceptionally crowded till supper made a diversion from the drawing room, but we got away about one, leaving the company then to keep it up as they liked & we hear they stayed till past 3 o'clock. I will send you what Newspapers I can giving you an account both of these festivities & the proceedings with respect to the Prisoners. We still set out on Wednesday 4th for Montreal, but it is doubtful we women shall go further. The Pirates are still troublesome & they say we should be in the way. Nobody speaks of any thing like danger & if we should find on arriving at Montreal that all is quiet I yet hope we may be allowed to proceed as I had much rather keep all together & besides am anxious to have seen all sights without delay.

47

I have not ventured, my dearest Mary, to write to Caroline, I hope & trust that all has gone well but in the uncertainty of this distance I cannot bear the thought of writing something which may be distressing to her at the moment it arrives, but I hope you will explain to her the cause of my silence, & repeat to her, again & again, how anxious I am for her & her dear children. Lambton was very stiff for a day or two after his fall, but he saved his head & no longer feels the effect of it & we are all well tho' George & Alice don't look as they did when we came from Howick.[65] *Pray give thousands of loves to Papa & all & good bye my dearest Mary.*

Yr. most affect.

Louisa

We have not yet received our things & I have great doubts whether they may not still be waiting at Cleveland Row.

Sir J. Colborne goes on to night to the Upper Province & both he & the Admiral, Sir C. Paget, will be with Lambton when he gets there.

WEDNESDAY, 4 JULY

We embarked on the *John Bull* Steamer about one o'clock. The Admiral set off about the same time in the *Medea* but did not reach Montreal so early as we did. The afternoon was excessively hot & sultry. There was a great deal of very vivid lightning all the evening, the effect of which was very beautiful, & we remained on deck watching it till the heavy rain obliged us to come down stairs. For some hours in the night the storm continued very violent & we found the cabins, which it was necessary to keep closed, dreadfully hot & close. The motion of the Steam boat also was most disagreeable. We reached Montreal by 6 o'clock.

Quebec

July 4th

My dearest Mary,

We set off this morning by the Steam-boat for Montreal, & I have not much time to spare, but as I hear a transport will sail to day for England I will at least write a few lines to tell you we are all well. We shall stay at Montreal till Monday, living in the steam-boat which is a very fine one, but too large to go higher up. The route afterwards is not positively settled, as it will depend upon the account from Sir John Colborne who went on two days ago. I trust however that we shall all go together. They propose our going up by the Ottawa & the Rideau Canal, which would show us a beautiful part of the Country, & avoid the thousand islands & all chance of Bill Johnson,[66] & then afterwards if all is quiet returning from Niagara by the St. Lawrence. We have lately had 2 or 3 desperately hot days & another violent thunderstorm, but I dare say it will change again soon, & at any rate while we are moving on the river we shall feel the heat less than on shore—it will also be such a respite getting away from company!—think of our having been yesterday 13 ladies at dinner in a party of 44. We should have had more ladies but several were unable to come. However I trust the list is now got through, & I hope we shall not have so much of them when we return. Lambton is seriously occupied all day, but I assure you our duties with the ladies are no sinecure, such people as they are! & such an affair that it is going from one to the other trying to speak to them all equally, & not knowing the least thing about any one of them. The dining room is happily very cool now that we are in the Assembly House & the library is above it, but by the time we have had the lights burning some little while, & that I have been slaving 3 or 4 hours, I get very hot, & have always a great "Ouf" to say after they are gone & I have done with them. By the bye, we hear the ball was much liked & the illuminations on board the ships wonderfully admired in spite of the rain. Every morsel of supper was cleared away & they drank 36 Dozn. of Champagne!

The Ellices go with us to Montreal & then I believe proceed to Beauharnois,[67] their own home. Charles & Caroline accompany us. I have not time, my dearest Mary, to write to any one else, but beg you will give my best love to Papa, my sisters & brothers. I should have had letters written before had I known of this transport but I only heard of it last night. I trust Caroline

is well & happy about her child & that we may soon hear of her.
Good bye my dearest Mary,

Yr. most affect.
Louisa

I will write from Montreal by New York if possible.

THURSDAY, 5 JULY
[In the morning] the weather was still unsettled & altho' the children & I crossed with my brother Charles (who had come to meet us) to the Island of St. Helens, we were overtaken by rain, & again a violent Thunderstorm in which we had some difficulty in crossing the stream to return to the Steamer. His landing at Montreal was deferred till the next day. The evening was fine & we rowed in the Admiral's barge after the dinner was over.

FRIDAY, 6 JULY
The next day was beautiful but very hot. We went on shore at 11 and ½. His reception was most satisfactory—more cordial & enthusiastic than at Quebec, which was particularly gratifying as it was expected that at Montreal, if any where, some feeling of dissatisfaction might be manifested on account of the mercy which had been extended to the prisoners in the Ordinances of June 26th. Nothing, however, of the sort appeared, & this city being much more populous than Quebec, the numbers of people in the streets were much larger, & the animation of the crowds who were assembled to witness his public entry much greater. We remained a few days at Montreal living on board the Steamer, during which he had constant interviews with the principal people of the place, both singly & in deputations. He also received addresses in public, held a Levee & attended a review which took place on the side of the Mountain above the town. The scenery being very advantageous & crowds of people covering the ground, the effect was very good. Besides all this he gave every day a large dinner to about 50 people on board the Steamer. The only moments of relaxation He had in the course of the day were after this was over in the Evg. We then rowed

about the river in the Admiral's barge & once or twice landed in the Island of St. Helens, which is a delightful spot & seems intended for a gentleman's Park. I believe these had been gardens & pleasure grounds when belonging to a Seigneur, but it is now the property of the Govt. The weather was extremely hot & we found it very oppressive both on shore & on board the Steamer, indeed the fatigue to Him in particular, attending this whole excursion, was excessive. Fire Flies were to be seen every Evg.

Montreal
July 8

My dearest Mary,
We arrived here at 6 o'clock on Thursday 5th after a passage of about 16 hours from Quebec. I think I never remember so hot a night or passed a much more uncomfortable one. The noise, motion & smell of the steamer were beyond belief, & tho' the dining & sitting cabins are more like fine rooms than cabins, the sleeping berths are very stuffy & confined. We had besides a violent thunder storm. We remained most of the evening on deck looking at the lightning which was most beautiful but terrific, tho' for a long time it was not accompanied by much thunder. At last however it came on in earnest with heavy rain & we were obliged to go down. In the night it was still worse, &, as is generally the case in this country, there was at the same time a violent gust of wind. The next day we had the same sort of weather. We were caught in the morning walking in Charles' island—St. Helens—& Lambton's landing was obliged to be deferred. Next day, however, Friday, it was very fine & he had a most brilliant reception. There were quantities of people out, & an immense deputation to present the address at Govt. House, who were all cordial & hearty beyond expectation. It had been supposed that the feeling might not be very good on account of the mercy shown to the Prisoners, but on the contrary, nothing could be more gratifying than everything that took place. All parties are delighted with Lambton's answer to the address, & the cheering at the review yesterday was, if possible still more enthusiastic

than at the landing. In short, Montreal which some people called disaffected, has surpassed Quebec in public demonstrations & it certainly is most satisfactory that it should be so, for on his first landing at the latter place Lambton was not known. Now, on the other hand, he has shown so decidedly what course of policy he means to pursue that the approbation, or otherwise, which he meets with, is not given in uncertainty.

Montreal is a much better town & altogether I should think a much more liveable place than Quebec. It has not the same magnificent view & situation as Quebec, but it seems much more pretty & enjoyable, & I like the thought of passing the winter here much better than at the other place. I am also pleased with the appearance of the house which has been taken for us. It is still occupied with Plasterers & Carpenters, but they promise its being finished within two months, & there are plenty of rooms to lodge us very comfortably, altho' there are no fine ones like the two we have at Quebec.

I am delighted to say that we are going on with Lambton to Niagara. He had despatches from Sir John Colborne last night saying that there was not the slightest risk in doing so, & I assure you, you may depend upon him. He is most cautious with respect to us & would not on any account take upon himself the responsibility of exposing us to the slightest alarm. We set out early on Tuesday 10th morning & we shall have two long days, but chiefly by water to Kingston. We shall there find Sir J. Colborne & proceed with him next day to Niagara where we expect to remain very comfortably 3 or 4 days. Sir. G. Arthur[68] will come there to meet Lambton who will thus be spared a further journey into the Province, & we shall come back here the way we came, perhaps stopping for a night at Beauharnois with Mr. Ellice, but that is only 14 miles from here. Charles & Caroline are quite well & accompany us on this tour. They have dined with us every day on board, but I am sorry to say not in comfort, for we have always had many strangers, & tho' it may perhaps be cooler here than in most places on shore, we have suffered most intensely from heat. Yesterday afternoon there was a very pretty review on the side of the mountain, but the only really pleasant thing we have done has been rowing by moonlight in the Admiral's barge. This was really delightful & perfectly beautiful. I could with pleasure have passed half the night, or the whole of it, in this way.

We are all well tho' rather oppressed with the heat in all we have to do. Lambton is quite wonderful, but then he is much gratified & pleased, as he ought to be, with the success of his visit here. He had looked upon it quite as a sort of crisis, & could not have hoped for a more favorable result.

Mary & all the children desire thousands of loves to you, but it is too hot & they have not plans to write—the same reasons will prevent my doing so to any one besides yourself, but I hope you will give my best love to Papa & all, & you may depend upon my writing again the very first opportunity. We expect to be here again about the 20th, but I don't know how that will suit for the New York Packet, so, if there should be a greater delay in hearing than you expect, you must not imagine that we have fallen in with Bill Johnson. You must also recollect that the greater part of the stories you will probably see in the News-papers about him, are pure invention, & that we have escorts & guards without end. Good bye my dearest dear Mary—my particular love to dear Caroline.

Yr. most affect.
Louisa

The Admiral, Sir C. Paget, goes with us poor man! He has very bad accounts of his Daughter who is I fear in a very bad way at Bermuda.

TUESDAY, 10 JULY

We got up at 4 & ½ & set off between 6 & 7 in the carriages to La Chine. The journey up the St. Lawrence was to be performed principally on the river by Steamers, but occasionally, where the navigation was interrupted by rapids, we had to proceed by land along the most dreadful roads I had ever encountered. He must have seen something like them in Russia but no where else. The saddle horses were taken with us & the children rode a great deal.

He set out with them from Cascades, but the rain soon drove him into the carriages. We had our English Chariot but were obliged to leave it behind on the second day. Luckily we had not much more occasion for it. The carriages of the country were uncouth looking vehicles, but more calculated for the roads we were travelling. They swung a great deal, but I did not think the one I went in afterwards, quite as rough as I expected. On this day our stations were to La Chine by land—to Cascades by the river—to Coteau du Lac by land, at which places he received an address, & at about 10 at night we arrived, after a long & fatiguing day, at Cornwall, where we slept.

There was here a Guard of Honours & people waiting to receive him in form, but heavy rain & a violent thunderstorm interfered very much with their arrangements. The accomodations at the Inn were very miserable, & we had a good deal of difficulty as George was taken very unwell on arriving. He was very ill for some hours, but got better & was nearly recovered next day.

Our party was a large one, consisting besides our own people & Charles & Caroline, of the Admiral & his suite. We did not get to bed till very late.

WEDNESDAY, 11 JULY

[We] were obliged to get up next morning at 3 in order to be off by daylight at 4 & $\frac{1}{2}$. The Girls rode in spite of much rain, & we proceeded in the carriage through a country of rough, woody scenery, without any particular beauty, to Dickenson's landing where we parted with the English carriage & embarked on board the Brockville Steamer. We stopped at Prescott & continued our voyage by the Thousand Islands, arriving at Kingston about 11 at night. Here we found a pretty good Inn & were comfortable. The children & I had some time to rest, as we remained till the middle of the next day, but He was out early in the morning inspecting the Docks, the Fort, Situation of the place &c. At 2 o'clock we embarked in the Cobourg Steamer on Lake Ontario. Our voyage by the Thousand Islands had been most prosperous, no appearance of Pirates or ill-disposed persons, but we heard afterwards that Bill Johnson, the most dreaded of these robbers, had been very near us. The Scenery of the 1000 Ids. has in it a great deal of calm beauty, but there is nothing grand except the size of the river, which one is scarcely aware of in passing between the Islands. A more favorable situation, however, could not well be imagined for a nest of pirates, as it would be nearly impossible to trace them through the innumerable Islands, all similar in appearance & affording endless places of concealment.

FRIDAY, 13 JULY

[We] arrived about 7 o'clock at Ft. Niagara (or Fort St. George) a small fort & town built at the entrance of the river Niagara into the lake. Here Sir John Colborne came on board, & we continued by the Steamer up the river through pretty woody scenery till we reached Queenston, where he landed with Sir John Colborne & proceeded on horseback, the children accompanying them in the same way. As I watched them from the Steamer, winding up the steep hill, the effect was very picturesque & pretty. Soon afterwards I followed in an open carriage with Caroline & Alice. The day was lovely & when we reached the top of the hill & Brock's Monument,[69][60] the views of the surrounding country to a great distance were very beautiful. (He used to say afterwards at Richmond that the view from the Star & Garter put him in mind of this, in small.) The road continues through a pretty wooded country to Niagara Falls where we arrived about one o'clock at the Clifton Hotel.

On approaching the Falls by this road no distant sight of them is caught, but on turning an eminence they burst into view immediately opposite in all their glory & magnificence—the most stupendous, sublime & beautiful spectacle in Creation. I cannot conceive that any other sight in the world can come near this, or that human imagination can form the faintest idea without beholding it, of what it is in reality. The eruption of a Volcano, I have since thought, might convey impressions nearly as striking. Possibly this might be the fact in point of terror & magnificence, but in Beauty the Falls of Niagara must be unrivalled. There seems to me to be a calmness in their sublimity, & at the same moment an overwhelming idea of Power that I can feel, but which I cannot describe. He said (in a letter) that no one but Milton could describe such a scene, & such is the truth. We were lost in admiration, wonder & delight. We had been told that we should be disappointed at first, & that it would require a little time to understand all the beauties of the scene, but such I do not find to be the case, altho' it is true that every hour one remained, one's admiration seemed to increase & the changes of every instant, in light & Colour & varied effect, offered an endless succession of enchantment. I felt that one could look or think on nothing else. I had not been prepared for such sensations of delight & could not have imagined that any outward impression of Nature had the power of producing such an effect. But it was positive happiness. In an instant the face of every thing was changed (in my feelings at least). Gloom & doubt seemed to disappear, difficulties vanished, & I could now admit pleasing hopes & anticipations in which till this moment I had never been able to indulge & which Alas! were not destined to be realized.

On reaching the Hotel I found Him already arrived & waiting for us. He had been received with military honours & a salute which he described as fine, within sight of the Falls, but this was over when I came & I can scarcely fancy that in such a scene one could have attention to spare for such circumstances, altho' in this case personal considerations rendered them to us remarkable.

Almost immediately after our arrival we set out walking to the Table Rock. Here I thought I could conceive the Deluge, & this impression returned upon me various times at different points of view. The Table Rock is said to be the spot from whence the view is finest, & perhaps on the whole it may be so, altho' there is a point on the American side which to me seemed even more stupendous, but it is scarcely possible to decide on a preference. The day was beautiful & the various & changing effects of light & sunshine more lovely than it is possible to conceive. From the Table Rock we went to the Hotel above the Falls, from whence there is some view of the Rapids which are also extremely fine & would be thought more of if all admiration was not so soon lost in that inspired by the Falls, which are here seen from above. They are magnificent in any point of view, but I prefer to this the situation of the Clifton Hotel, where we were lodged, & which is placed just opposite to the American Falls, so close that the vibration is sensibly felt & appears something like the motion of a Steam-boat. It is also much exposed to the spray & foam, when the wind sets toward it, but the view of the Falls opposite & of the whole Amphitheatre formed by the Horse-Shoe Fall is perfectly beautiful. It was with difficulty I could leave the Verandah or the window for an instant.

We had a very large party to dinner on this day. Sir John Colborne & Sir G. Arthur, who had also come to meet Him, being both present with their suites.

Clifton Hotel, Niagara
just opposite the Falls
Saty. July 14

My dearest Mary,
How I wish I could bring you here! I have scarcely, except for my own sake, felt such a wish before, but now for yours, how I long to have you enjoying this unequalled Spectacle! It has gone far towards reconciling me to our exile, & I really believe if every thing is settled for our return next summer, I shall almost consider that this one sight has repaid us for the sacrifice of coming. I cannot conceive what people mean by talking of disappointment. When the view first opened upon me on driving down to the hotel I was in perfect rapture, & this feeling is still encreased when you walk on the Table Rock about ¼ mile from here. It is true that the other hotel above the falls has scarcely a view of the cascade, tho' a very fine one of the rapid & river above, & perhaps it is this which has caused the feeling of disappointment I have heard so generally expressed as to the first impression, but I can hardly fancy even that, because I think it is quite evident, even from this point, that you can have no notion what the fall of the water is, but that you must be persuaded that there is something sublime below you. Standing on the Table Rock, which is the finest point I have yet seen, the idea I had was that I could imagine the deluge, & that I beheld the waters let

loose to cover & swallow up the earth. The day was beautiful, & the various effects of the sunshine, the rainbow in the foam & the different tints of the water, all more lovely one than another —I can never be tired of looking at them. After speaking of Niagara it is hard to mention any thing else, otherwise I should say we had been much pleased with a great deal of the scenery of the St. Lawrence as we came up. The Montreal Islands are exceptionally pretty & the entrance to this river & the view above Queenston from Brock's Monument magnificent. We had a great deal of rain on the first day of our journey & a terrible thunder storm at Cornwall where we slept the first time, but excepting that I must say our journey was very prosperous. If you have a good map of Canada you may trace our route from Montreal to La Chine by land—to Cascades by water—from there to Coteau du Lac by land—& then the remainder of the first day's journey by water to Cornwall, where we took up our quarters for a very short night in a very miserable inn. We started the next morning at ½ past 4, went 12 miles by land over the most dreadful road that can be conceived, the children riding in spite of very heavy rain which Mr. Cavendish⁷⁰ however was pleased to call a passing shower—it has been a joke against him ever since—but through very pretty Country & by the Long Sault rapid which is very beautiful, to Dickenson's landing. There we got into the Steamers for the whole day, had no more rain, passed Prescott, the Thousand Islands—the supposed haunts of the Pirates, & better hiding places for them could not I should think be found—but did not arrive at Kingston till 11 at night. There was then a question whether we should land or go on board the Steamer, on which we were to proceed next day, but it was luckily decided for landing, for we made ourselves very comfortable at the Inn on the shore & did not leave it till two the next day, so we had plenty of time to rest. Lambton was indeed up early, inspecting Forts, Docks etc., but he is very well & seems quite equal to the work he has undertaken, but which I assure you is no slight one, even with respect to bodily fatigue. From Kingston we came on to Queenston. We entered the river Niagara about 7 in the morning having passed a disagreeable night on board a *very stinking Steamer, but we were lucky that it was the only one. Lake Ontario is an immense body of water looking like a Sea, & can be very rough, tho' we had a smooth passage. There was nothing remarkable in the part of the coast near it which we could see. Sir John Colborne joined us at Queenston & Sir G. Arthur arrived here soon after we did. Nothing can be more favorable than the accounts of the country. The 1500 men who had been reported to Sir J. Colborne have dwindled to 50, & even they I believe have disappeared & the country is perfectly quiet. We shall not however be back at Montreal quite so soon as we expected. We are so delighted with this place that we shall be glad to spend a few days here, & I believe Sir G. Arthur wishes Lambton to go to Toronto, which will also prolong our journey some days. However despatches are, I hope, going to England from here, & I am quite willing to be longer away, provided I do not think you are making yourself uneasy at the thoughts of our travelling in what you imagine to be a disturbed country.*

The whole party are gone to day to see Fort Erie, & we get a look at the Lake, but as I believe they will find nothing very remarkable when they get there, I was lazy & have preferred remaining quietly in this most beautiful place with Alice, whom I find a delightful companion when she is left alone with me. We had had a long day yesterday, & instead of a quiet evening at the end of it, 40 people to dinner, so that I was quite glad to find myself alone for a few hours. I believe I told you that Sir C. Paget was to accompany us, but I must add that I delight in him. I think he is the kindest person I ever saw, tho' I hear he can be very hot. He has several people with him, we have all the A.D.C., the Doctor, Mr. Smythe the Artist,[71] & Mr. C. Buller who is very unwell & takes no care of himself. He is not much thrown in my way, but he is a good deal improved upon me. He seems very obliging & goodnatured, which I did not expect, & I think all the people with us like him very much. His brother[72] is insufferably conceited, but as I have never had occasion to speak 5 words to him since we arrived at Quebec, he only offends my eyes when I happen to cast them upon him.

I will now, my dearest Mary, put an end to my letter. I cannot afford at Niagara to give more time to writing, so I must again beg you will ask my sisters to be satisfied with my kindest love *through you, but I dare say Mary will write before we go. Thousands & thousands of loves to Papa & all. I trust we shall find news, & good news of you all, when we return to Montreal, but the Gt. Western put us so much in advance that we have had a long, long interval of silence.*

Yr. most affect.
Louisa

Monday 16th
We went across yesterday evg. to the American side & walked round Goat Island. There is one point of view in ascending which I think beyond every thing, but in general this side is most beautiful.

We go on Wednesday to Toronto & after passing the Sunday with Mr. Ellice at Beauharnois expect to be at Montreal on Monday 23rd.

SATURDAY, 14 JULY
[The] next day He & most of the party went to Fort Erie. It was a long & toilsome expedition over roads in bad carriages on a very hot, sultry day, & they did not return till past 7, when we had a party of 44 to dinner. I did not accompany them, but from all I heard the fatigue must have been great—much too great for him, occupied as he was by business of the most exciting nature without time even for natural rest. He was always up early, if possible—one morning as early as 4 o'clock—writing letters & despatches for England.

SUNDAY, 15 JULY
We dined at 4 without many strangers, & being very desirous of seeing the Falls from the American side, it was decided on the instant that we should go, & without [making] preparations beforehand we took the small Ferry boat & crossed over. The boat crosses so close under the Falls that the motion is rather

startling & gives an idea of danger, altho' I heard of no accidents having ever occurred. It is also so completely under the spray that it is necessary to have some covering as a protection from the wet. It was immediately after landing, on ascending the steps of what is called the staircase, that we came to the point which struck me as so infinitely sublime. The water rushes from above with tremendous & overpowering force & a noise which is almost deafening. The idea of the Deluge again filled my imagination, & the impressions of irresistible & overwhelming power were awful & astounding. No where did I experience these sensations so vividly as on this spot, but, as a whole, the view from the Table Rock of the Two Falls (the American & the Horse Shoe) is more entire & complete. We proceeded to Goat Island, crossing the very remarkable bridge which is built over the Rapids, & walked round the Island which stands between the two falls & is full of beauty, but we were much hurried in our visit & never had an opportunity of returning. Some of the party crossed to the Tower built on the edge of the Horse Shoe Fall & climbed to the top of it. The effect of the bright English Uniforms in the evening light, as I watched them from a little distance was picturesque, & remarkable, considering the circumstances in which they were seen. (I think He crossed to the tower but did not go to the top of it.)

We did not get home till dusk & found ourselves a good deal exhausted with the exertions of the evening, & the great changes from the heat in walking on shore, to the showers of wet spray which covered us as we crossed the river under the Falls.

It was reckoned something of a bold measure to cross in this way, He & his Staff in full Uniform among the Americans, & I believe, if much had been said about it, or he had regularly consulted Sir J. Colborne & others, that he would have been advised against it. We had heard a great deal on arriving of the bad spirit which prevailed across the Frontier but we met with nothing but civility—people even taking off their hats as we passed, an unusual mark of respect among the Americans, but they were flattered, I believe, at the confidence he manifested & the result proved that he was right in going among them at once, without sign of doubt or hesitation. We heard afterwards that as soon as it was known we were gone across, our return had been watched for with some anxiety at Niagara.

MONDAY, 16 JULY

The Admiral & my brother Charles went to see the Welland Canal. He was to have made this excursion but was not well in the morning & obliged to remain at home. It was not surprising that he was knocked up with all he had to do & when he was obliged to give in for a short interval He never allowed himself sufficient time to recover but resumed his exertions before the attack was by any means dispelled. This was particularly the case at the present time, & it was long (if at all during the remainder of his stay in Canada) before he recovered the excursion to Fort Erie & the fatigues & excursions of this visit to Niagara & the Upper Provinces.

TUESDAY, 17 JULY 73

The 43rd Regt.[73] was stationed here & encamped in a most picturesque situation above the Falls. On the 17th it was reviewed. The ground chosen for the occasion, at a short distance, was extremely pretty & very favorable for the manœuvers which were so executed as to obtain great praise from the Military persons present, & even to afford much interest to ignorant spectators. The sight attracted a great number of Americans who came over from Buffalo &c. The Officer highest in rank on the Frontier, Major [Young] was received by Him & attended to all the morning with great civility, & was requested to stay for dinner & a dance afterwards with as many of his countrymen as he might like to invite & who might wish to remain.[74] About 30 (I think) accepted the invitation & more would have done so but there were difficulties about their arrangements for returning. Those who staid appeared much gratified by the civilities they met with. We dined at 4 o'clock, sitting down about 200, the company consisting, besides the Americans, of people from the neighbourhood—Officers &c. At the Dessert he gave the President's health, & as Mr. Buller says "a million of money would have been a cheap price for the single glass of wine which Lord Durham drank to the health of the American President." It was the first occasion on which any attempt towards cordiality had been made on the part of a British Commander, & the result completely answered his expectations. From that moment a marked change took place in the feeling of the People of the United States, & for the first time good will & a friendly spirit seemed to prevail among them towards the English of the Colonies. These dispositions were still further encouraged on His return to Quebec. He set apart a day for receiving all those who came with satisfactory references & showed further civilities to each as prolonged their stay.

WEDNESDAY, 18 JULY
We left Niagara to our great regret; we could willingly have passed there a whole summer, but our visit had not been arranged as a party of pleasure, & he had given us all the time he could afford in the execution of the great objects in which he was engaged. We had truly enjoyed the 5 days we had spent there [&] they would have been still more delightful could they have been passed more quietly with no object to interfere with the charms & wonders of the place, but surrounded as he was & occupied with business & the duties of society, this was impossible. The weather too was excessively hot & all exertion overpowering. He never could find an opportunity of returning to the Table Rock, & we, even altho' we were anxious to see it again, failed in accomplishing our wishes. The morning on which we went was beautiful. The girls, George &c. set off very early on horseback, but he went with me & Alice in a carriage. We started soon after 7 & on our way stopped to see The Whirlpool, a remarkable spot on the river Niagara, which turns suddenly round making an elbow & forming a deep gulf & whirlpool. We were much pleased with the beauty of the scene, but were forced to hurry away from it. At Queenston we embarked again on the Steamer accompanied by Sir John Colborne & his Staff. The Admiral, being unwell, had been forced to remain at the Falls. At Niagara, at the mouth of the river, we stopped. The children & those who had rode

63

came on board, & He received two large Deputations with Addresses on the deck of the Steamer. We then entered again upon Lake Ontario, along the shores of which it had been intended he should proceed in order to visit Hamilton & see part of the country in that district. It was found, however, that there would not be sufficient time for all that had been proposed, & it was therefore decided that He should only land at Pt. Dalhousie to inspect the mouth of the river leading to the Welland Canal. This He did, in spite of a severe attack in the head which had seized him soon after he came on board. He saw all that was necessary (with Sir J. Colborne) but suffered dreadfully afterwards, & was so ill when he approached Toronto that it was necessary to keep off the Steamer & delay his landing for half an hour while He endeavoured, by a hot bath for his feet, & such remedies as could be given for the moment to palliate the suffering so as to enable him to get thro' the ceremonies of the public reception that awaited him at Toronto. Having thus waited till the last moment, he dressed & went on shore, but in a very unfit state for so great an effort. He had such resolution & energy that He would never give in where he thought the object required the exertion. On this occasion he seemed so extremely unwell that I was quite alarmed for the consequences. He landed between 4 & 5 & was received with every demonstration of respect & rejoicing. Crowds of people attended & followed him with loud acclamations. Arches of evergreens & displays of Flags were arranged on his passage & the soldiers in the town drawn up in military [ranks] at the landing place or lining the streets, Sir George Arthur receiving Him on his arrival & proceeding with him in procession to the House of Assembly, where he conducted him into the principal room (that of the Council, I think.) Here he received an address, a number of ladies being present to witness the proceedings. After this another address was presented & read by the Mayor, outside on the steps of the Building, to which he returned an answer & made a short speech with great effect. From thence He drove round the town, still in cortege, & at last arrived at the Govt. House where we were to be lodged for the night.

Sir George Arthur had made every possible arrangement for our comfort but the fatigues of the day were not yet over, for after a short interval of rest we had to dress for dinner, which was given in a large new room just finished, to a party of 60 people. The dinner was long & tedious & at the dessert he had twice to make a speech, once in returning thanks for his own health given by Sir G. Arthur, & again in giving that of Sir George. So ended a day of frightful fatigue, the effects of which he felt for a long time, the only softening circumstances being the comfort of Sir G. Arthur's house which was furnished like an English one & where we had rooms as comfortable as if we had been at home, which we found very enjoyable after the Inns & Steamers.

THURSDAY, 19 JULY
Next day he was rather better but did not go out, altho' he was employed in perhaps a more fatiguing manner in holding a Levee & giving interviews to numerous persons who were anxious to see him. I saw a few ladies & then took a drive about town with the girls & Caroline under the guidance of Capt. Arthur. The morning was very fine & we saw Toronto to great advantage. It is in general spoken of [as] a dull place, but the numbers of people who had come in from the surrounding country, & the animation that prevailed in the town did not admit of such an impression upon us. We were, on the contrary, rather struck with the appearance of the streets which seemed to be better built & to consist of better houses than any place we had seen. There also seemed to be some pleasant houses & gardens looking towards the Lake. The shores are flat & the country seems to afford no particular feature of interest, but still, the large extent of water & the richness of the country have a pleasing effect.

In the afternoon we again set off, leaving Toronto in nearly the same order as we had left it—in open carriages, the soldiers drawn out & people assembled as before. The weather had been fine tho' very hot all morning & altho' it had become rather overcast it was quite fair when we started & no one seemed to anticipate the sudden burst of rain which overtook us before we reached the Port, & fell as if from a Water Spout. All those who accompanied us on horseback were drenched. A tremendous storm of thunder & lightening followed. We had all been hurried on board the steamer as fast as possible, & tho' most of those who had attended our departure made the best of their way to find places of shelter on shore, a considerable number of persons (a Deputation & others) were detained on board above an hour before they could find a tolerable interval of fair weather to return. As soon as they left us we got underway, the Chief Justice of Upper Canada, Mr. Robinson,[75] accompanying us in order that Lambton might take the opportunity of having some conversation with him. The rain cleared off & the girls & I staid till late in the evening on deck, altho' the air was chilly, forming a great contrast to the heat of the morning. It was at all times fresh on the water & we had experienced nearly as great changes of temperature the day before, in coming from Niagara, where we had found it extremely hot in the morning, again so on arriving at Toronto, while on the lake it was more than cool. We passed an uncomfortable night in the Steamer, having been obliged to close the cabin, far more than was pleasant on account of the rain & another violent Thunder Storm which appeared to pass very near us.

FRIDAY, 20 JULY

At 11 o'clock we arrived at Kingston, where He again landed to receive an address, but did not remain long on shore. We then proceeded through the 1000 Islands, steering more towards the right bank & passing Well's Island where we saw the wreck of the *Sir Robert Peel*,[76] the Steamer which had been destroyed by American Pirates soon after our arrival in Canada. We also looked into French Creek, the great nest of the Pirates on the American Shore. The afternoon was showery, but we remained a great deal on deck. We admired the pretty situation of Brockville as we passed by, & arrived before 8 o'clock at Prescott. Here we parted with Chief Justice Robinson & changed into another Steamer, for which however, we waited for some time.

66

Next morning, having reached Dickenson's Landing we left the Steamer at 7 o'clock, & went on board a large bateau (as it is called in the country) in which we rowed down the Long Sault rapid. As is shewn by the name, this rapid is of considerable length, but the descent is very gradual & I should scarcely have perceived anything unusual in our passage. At Cornwall we found another Steamer which took us to the Coteau du Lac. Here again another address was presented, & we then removed again into a large Bateau, called here a Durham boat, which carried us through some very considerable rapids, particularly those of the Cedars & Cascades. In these the motion of the water is exceeding strong, & great dexterity is required in the management of the helm, as the slightest inadvertance on the part of the steerers would cause the loss of the boat & all on board. The scenery in this part of the river is extremely pretty. On approaching Beauharnois, where we arrived in the afternoon, Edward Ellice came out to meet us in a small Indian Canoe rowed by 3 Indians & a French Canadian who took the lead & gave a succession of French boat songs to which the Indians joined in chorus, marking the time as they struck the water with their short oars. The Canoe was narrow & long, holding but one, or at most two, persons besides the rowers who sat in the bottom of the boat. The effect of the whole thing was unlike any thing we had ever seen & amused us exceedingly. The girls &c. were much pleased at going about in this Canoe during the two days we passed with Mr. & Mrs. Ellice." The cottage in which they lived, & which in general was occupied by the Agent, was so small that they were obliged to remove out of it themselves in order to accomodate us. They took the greatest pains to make us comfortable & succeeded very well, the weather being fine. At a worse season the house could scarcely have been habitable, altho' Mrs. Ellice had contrived with a little English Furniture & good arrangement to make it look very nice for the time. We found the weather cooler on this day than it had been since we left Quebec. Here at last we had the prospect of a quiet day & a little rest of which He was in great want. Still, he had Deputations & people to receive, & on

Monday was so unwell that his departure was delayed till next day."[78] 79

He was rather better & at 12 o'clock we went on board the Steamer which took us to Lachine, from where we went by land to Montreal. Alice was in the carriage with us. The girls, George &c. rode. Again we had torrents of rain on entering the town & were obliged to hurry to our old quarters on board the *John Bull* anchored in the middle of the stream. We remained two days at Montreal. On the first of these He went on shore, visited the Catholic Seminary & distributed prizes to the pupils, still continuing to see crowds of people on board till the moment of his departure. By this time, however, He was so worn out by the constant fatigues he had been undergoing that a little respite became indispensable, & altho' it had been proposed that He should extend his tour by the Eastern townships (where he would have had some fatigue travelling by land) it was now decided that he should relinquish this scheme for the present. Having therefore dined at 4, we took leave of Caroline & Charles & left Montreal about 5 & ½. The evening was delightful & the river so clear that the stars were reflected in it—a beautiful effect which we had never witnessed before.

We passed Sorel & anchored about 11 o'clock. As soon as it was daylight (about 4 o'clock) we proceeded again & arrived at Quebec about 11 a.m. The weather, which had been cooler for a day or two while we were at Beauharnois, was again very hot.

We were not sorry after our journeyings (altho' the expedition had been a most interesting one, & Niagara alone would make up for the voyage across the Atlantic) to find ourselves once again at home. The servants had been employing themselves, during our absence, in getting the house into order & we were now very comfortable. The furniture was of the plainest description, & in the children's rooms there was nothing beyond common necessaries, but the rooms were airy & pleasant, & in ours we had every thing we wanted. The Library, a large room with windows both ways & a beautiful view on one side upon the

St. Lawrence, made a very agreeable sitting room. It was the only one, but we found it quite sufficient. It contained a good collection of books & among them many works of History, Biography, Travel &c. which were a great resource where there was little of any thing new to be had.

On our return we began to fall into a more settled way of life & to accomodate our habits to the arrangements of the situation. Having now seen most of the principle people at dinner, two days in the week were found sufficient for large parties. On the others we were more to ourselves. (I find it put down that on the 30th we dined for the first time since our arrival in Quebec without the addition of a stranger.) We always found it answered much better, as the weather was still very hot, to dine early (at 4 o'clock) & to go out afterwards. By this means we had always two good hours for a drive before dusk, as the party separated immediately when dinner was over. This shortened the time of our duties to strangers, without being less satisfactory to them. They were pleased at coming but ill at their ease, & when the party naturally broke up in this way it was equally agreeable to them & much more so to us. It was certainly a great deal better for Him. He was much less likely to be interrupted & deprived of the opportunity of getting some air than when he attempted to go out before dinner. The evenings, too, were delightful. We often took long drives in the environs of Quebec which are beautiful, or went to the plains of Abraham where the views in the setting sun over the mountains & the magnificent St. Lawrence were quite lovely. He used to go with me in the open Barouche. The girls & George generally rode after us [with] one or two of the Aide-de-Camps or the suite accompanying us. When we returned we had Tea & passed the remainder of the Evening either alone, or with one or two of those who had been with us. They too however left us early. We saw less now habitually of the suite. Some were occasionally absent & many had formed acquaintances with the people of the place & were often away. On the Company days, however, they were all present.

He continued, in pursuance of the course begun at Niagara, to show great attentions to the Americans. All those who arrived with respectable references, & many at this season extended their pleasure Tours as far as Quebec, shared his civilities. We were at home to receive them regularly once a week, & the day being known, their stay was generally arranged so as to include one of these Evenings. Besides this, we saw others at dinner, perhaps those who were more particularly recommended, or those whose time did not suit the regular Evenings. Among these I find mentioned a Genl. Houston[79] (who had served in the Texas War), a Judge from New York (His name I forget), Genl. Patterson[80] & two Daughters, & Mr. Picard (a lawyer, I think, or writer, & said to be a clever man whom Mr. Buller had met somewhere). He dined with us at one of the smaller dinners & drove with us afterwards to Lorette—a very hot close Evening with much bright lightening.

By the beginning of the month the Admiral, whom we had left ill at Niagara, had returned. He dined with us on [August] the 2nd and on the 6th removed into the house to stay. He had sent away the *Cornwallis* & hoistened his Flag in the *Inconstant*; but, of course, being confined in the Frigate, He, who was always hospitable & kind, besides having a great liking for Sir Charles Paget, invited him to come & live with us. This he did; a sitting room being arranged for him to receive his visitors, & every thing so settled that he could find himself perfectly independent. He still went on board the *Inconstant* to give his dinners, but at other times He saw a good deal of him & his nephew, Ld. Clarence Paget, who had arrived in his ship a short time before.

We all got on with the Admiral uncommonly well. He took to the children very much. Mary & Emily used to play to him & he seemed quite fond of little Alice whose progress as she grew up, he said he should watch with interest. Poor Man! not many months after this he was no more. He used to talk with great affection of his own daughters at home. One of them was in very bad health & at one time, soon after he arrived he had very bad accounts of her. Afterwards she was better & he seemed very much relieved.

My dearest Mary,

*You will be glad to hear that we are safely returned from
our expedition, having explored Bill Johnson's haunts, French
Creek, Buffalo, & landed in America without having encountered any enemy—or met with any thing but kindness & civility.
Toronto outdid all other places, & the pains Sir G. Arthur took
to make us comfortable in the first English house I have seen
since we left England, are not to be described. The only draw-
back has been that Lambton was at last fairly knocked up &
suffered a very severe attack. However he is now better having
been obliged to take two quiet days at Mr. Ellice's from where
we arrived this morning. I have not time to tell you much of the
latter part of the expedition, but I would not lose this opportunity of sending a line, as there is an Officer going to New York
who will arrive in time for the return of the* Royal William
*which we hope is by this time arrived. I trust it brings letters at
last for us, but there was a large bag arrived this morning with
news as late as June 16th & not a line for any one of us. I cannot
tell you how disappointed I was, as the last letters I have received
were of the 31st May &* 1st June with the improved *account of
Mary Barrington it is true, but still such a one as left us very
anxious to hear again. I suppose you will have left town when
this reaches you, but really I wish you would have some enquiries
made as to how our letters are sent. I strongly suspect that the
Colonial Office is the worst channel, & am much inclined to believe it would be better to trust to the Post to New York.*

*Lambton has given up for the present his intention of visiting
the Eastern Townships. He will be able to do it equally well
when he returns here, & tho' we have all enjoyed the excursion
beyond all expectation, we shall not be sorry to have a little rest
in our own house which I hope will now be quite comfortable.
We leave this the day after to morrow, & shall be at Quebec
next day. We are all quite well. Alice has borne the heat & the
travelling wonderfully. To be sure the Steamboats are not fatiguing to her as she always sleeps as if she were in her own bed, but*

she has often been disturbed at unusual hours. However she is looking much better than she was when we set out. We left the poor Admiral sick at the Falls of Niagara, but I hope he will soon join us again & Mr. Buller remained at Niagara—at the mouth of the river—having been so ill with the Asthma at the hotel under the spring of the falls that he could not stay there.

I shall be very busy to morrow with Mr. Ellice about the arrangement of the house, to say nothing of 3 Nunneries which I fear will insist on a visit, & to judge by a specimen we had at Quebec, that is not a slight affair—but as soon as we are settled again I will try & go back to what I have not had time to write about. Pray give thousands of loves to Papa & all. I have written in such a hurry that I have said nothing I wanted, & have wasted my time & paper without telling you any thing, but I think you will excuse me. Good bye my dearest Mary.

Yr. most affect.
Louisa

Quebec
Augst. 9th

My dearest Mary,
I have lately written to you on such sudden notices that I know I have neglected saying to you a great many of the things I wished. It is however so hard to write back, as to read back in the case of Newspapers, & I am puzzled to know what to return to. After all, I can only have missed things relating to one journey which interested me at the time, but were probably not much worth thinking of afterwards. By the bye, I must tell you that Lambon received three days ago, for the first time, a package of Newspapers beginning the end of April, but not coming down to a late date. They had been sent by the Colonial Office by the Halifax packet, & there they remained till the other day when the Malabar brought them. We are now in hourly expectation of receiving the letters by the Gt. Western & I have been waiting for their arrival to write, as when one knows there is something on the road of a much later date than what one has already received, one cannot write with satisfaction for the want of it. How-

ever we must now do so as Capt. Bagot, who takes the despatches,
must go to day in order to reach New York in time for her return
on the 16th. If by any chance you should still be in London you
will like to see Capt. Bagot,[81] *he is a son of Ldy. Harriet's, &*
a great friend of George's & now goes home on his promotion
having come out 1st Lieut. of the Medea. *He was with us on our*
tour of the Upper Provinces & will be able to tell you any thing
you like about this country.

I have been very near writing to you to look out for a maid
to send out to me before the winter, but I hope we shall be able
to go on without changing till we come home. My maid does not
turn out useful, & Mary's, who is, seemed so likely to be entirely
disabled by illness, that at one time I did not know what we
should do. However I am happy to say that she is getting much
better than one could have expected, & I hope I shall be able to
stir up mine sufficiently for the time, though I should not think
of keeping her forever in case Sophie[82] *should not return. I men-*
tion all this that you may keep your ears open in case you should
hear of any thing very desireable, & that you may know there is
a possibility of my having to write for a person. As to getting any
one here I should think it entirely out of the question.

We continue to have very hot weather with changes as usual
every two or three days. I must however acknowledge that we
have been out every evg. & that the greater number of them
have been delightful. Dining at 4 o'clock has made the whole
difference to comfort in our way of life—instead of struggling
on ages in the evening we now get the whole dinner over, even a
large party soon after 6, & go out & do as we please afterwards.
We have also nearly got through the Quebec people, & have had
a great deal more peace & comfort. The Admiral is now living
in our house, having sent his ship, the Cornwallis, *to Halifax, &*
shifted his flag on board the Inconstant. *He goes on board to give*
his dinners, & has a sitting room of his own here which makes
him quite independent, though indeed we are all so fond of him
that we never could see too much of him. His nephew, Lord
Clarence, I am sorry to say has been very ill & still looks fright-
fully weak. He is going away today in the Pearl (?). *We have*

not seen so much of him, but there is something very pleasing &
hearty in his manner, & I feel sorry for his family that his health
should be so bad.

I have nothing particular to tell you my dearest Mary, now
that we are established in our regular life here. By the bye, I
must tell you that Dethier is going away! such a relief! & I
trust that we shall now have every thing on a much more com-
fortable footing. Edward Ellice has also given up the concern.
To say the truth he was a little selfish about it, & not choosing
to look after the arrangements when he might have been useful.[83]
L. has been obliged to put it in the hands of another person. Mr.
Villiers[84] *has now undertaken it & I believe will do it very*
zealously & very well.

Pray give thousands & thousands of loves to Papa & all &
good bye my dearest Mary.

Yr. most affect.
Louisa

We are all well.

Quebec
Augst. 10*th*

My dearest Mary,
The departure of the Gt. Western *is delayed & I have time to*
thank you for the long letter I received by it yesterday just as the
bag was made up. I was much obliged to you for writing bit by
bit. I think it is much the pleasantest way at such a distance, &
what signifies it if there is a little contradiction in different parts
of the letter. I was very sorry that I had not adhered to this plan
during our tour, but there would have been a little difficulty in
managing it. I trust I may consider the last news of dear little
Mary as satisfactory, but I do not feel happy at the account you
give in your letter to me—poor Caroline too! how is she? She
must be worn out by such painful anxiety—it is equally bad also
for you, & I did not leave you strong but you never mention
your own health.

I am very much vexed at this business of Mr. Turton, & cannot
help thinking Ld. Melbourne is shabby about it. He certainly

knew when he went that he was not going on a party of pleasure
& ought to have been prepared for his appointment here, tho'
Lambton had compromised the matter so far as to yield the point
of his official appointment by the Govt. at home. I hope the storm
about him may have blown over, as nothing fresh has been done
here to excite it, but it is an annoying affair when otherwise every
thing would be going on so well.

I long to hear from you again but I fear we shall have no news
later than the Gt. Western *for a long time. Mr. Duncombe*[85] *is*
not yet arrived. I will now bid you good bye as I have nothing
particular to add. I send this by a groom who is going home
direct, as there is no new bag for the Gt. Western. *Thousands of*
loves to all.

Yr. most affect.
Louisa

MONDAY, 16 AUGUST

The *Medea* arrived bringing Sir Colin Campbell[86] & Sir Charles
Fitzroy,[87] Governors of Nova Scotia & Prince Edward's Island.
Sir Colin was accompanied by his Daughter. They remained at
Quebec till the 18th when they set off with Him in the *John Bull*
for Montreal to attend the races. The Admiral also accompanied
him & he took George. They set off at two & stopped at Sir John
Colborne's at Sorel on their way. Not having being quite well
the week before, I did not accompany him on this excursion. The
girls remained with me, but went with him in the *John Bull* as
far as the Chaudière, where He stopped to see the falls. They
rowed home in the Evg. in the Gig. He returned from Montreal
on the 22nd. While there He had been extremely unwell. The
heat of the sun had been excessive, & having been much exposed
to it, he suffered in consequence a kind of bilious attack which
weakened him very much. The weather, tho' still beautiful, was
beginning to alter a little. It was still nearly as hot as ever in the
middle of the day, but sometimes it turned a little cold towards
the Evg. Even while he was away we had begun to think of
changing the dinner hour that we might go out earlier. One day
we did this for the sake of crossing the river to Pt. Levi. We sent

over their horses for Mary & Emily[88] & Mr. Villiers drove me
with the Canadian ponies (he had bought at Toronto) in [the]
poney carriage. The views of Quebec, Montmorenci & the Isle
of Orleans from this side are beautiful. I had once before crossed
over to take a walk, but only once I think, & the girls had rode
there, but He never once landed on the opposite side altho' he
had often talked of doing so, as of seeing many other places
which he had never the opportunity of doing. At Montreal He
had been joined by Mr. Duncombe whom he had been expecting
some time, & who came back with him & remained with us. The
day He returned was a very hot one. We had a large dinner with
the Admiral, Govs. &c. In the Evg. there was a very fine Aurora
Borealis, & the effect of it on the beautiful scenery of the St.
Lawrence, with the shipping &c. was quite lovely. We had often
these appearances & used to watch them, with the moon & stars,
from the windows of the Library with great enjoyment.

Quebec
Augst. 17*th*

My dearest Mary,
I have now received by the Halifax Mail your letters of June
21st & 30th, which tho' of an older date than those of the Gt.
Western were still most welcome. Mr. Duncombe's is now, I
should think, the only one missing, but he has not yet made his
appearance. I cannot say how much I feel for the dreadful anxi-
ety you have all had to undergo on account of poor little Mary
Barrington, or how anxious I myself still feel for further ac-
counts of her. I hope & trust there is nothing left behind this
terrible illness but the weakness which a child will soon recover,
& I trust the next letters will tell me that you are all gone to
Howick, but after the Gt. Western it will be some time before
we receive any newer intelligence.
*   I have nothing very particular to tell you at present, but I*
write—I believe by New York—that you may not pass a longer
interval without hearing than is unavoidable on account of the
different modes of conveyance. The arrival of the Gt. Steamer,
when it does take place, is delightful, but it deranges the regular

76

routine & is a little tantalizing in some respects.

Lambton goes to morrow to Montreal for the races but has excused me & the girls from accompanying him. Mary & Emily are as glad to remain here as I am, or else I would have gone, but the house is not yet ready to receive us, & living on board the Steamer as we did before, with perhaps 30 or 40 people to dinner on board every day, altho' the accomodations are very good, is still a bore—& would be more so now that the days are getting shorter, & that we can less depend upon constantly living on deck. We shall therefore remain here with a quiet little party & do as we please. Our places in the Steamer are entirely filled up by the Admiral & the two Governors of Halifax & P. Edward's Isld., Sir Colin Campbell & Sir Charles Fitzroy, who arrived yesterday, with their people.

Edward Ellice has been here for a day to assist in the new arrangement of affairs in the House, but he has given over the charge of it to Mr. Villiers who takes great pains & seems to devote his whole time to the business. He is to settle all that remains to be done during Lambton's absence, & I hope at last we shall be comfortable but there have been great abuses to reform, & I individually shall not be quite well off, as I have heard unsatisfactory things about my maid, & I fear I shall never like her again, even if she does remain with me till I go home. The Housekeeper however turns out very well which is a good thing.

Lambton was not very well for a few days which did not surprise me, but I think he is better again. On the whole he thinks this climate agrees with him. There falls a great deal of rain, but the air is particularly pure & dry—see the tin roofs—& I believe it is a wholesome place if people can be on their guard against the sudden changes. It is bad for some cases of rheumatism, but I don't hear particular complaints of it for any thing else.

We have races here in little more than a fortnight, Sept. 3rd, & we hope that when Lambton comes back the middle of next week, he will be able to persuade Charles & Caroline to return with him & stay for them. We always like to have them, &

when we have company you have no idea how useful, how orna-
mental, & how much admired she is. To be sure, she & Mary,
& I think I may add Emily, look like creatures of another race
among people here. Pray give thousands & thousands of loves
to Papa & all. How good it was of him to write to Mary &
Alice! Good bye my dearest Mary.

Yr. most affect.
Louisa

THURSDAY, 23 AUGUST

The day after He came back, the Admiral took leave of us in the
evening. We parted with him with great regret. There had never
been the shadow of a difficulty among us, & those who were well
acquainted with him said they had seldom seen him so comfortable & happy. He had cooperated most cordially & efficiently
with L. in all the public business which they had had together
and He found the want of him very much after he was gone. We
watched him next morning as he sailed in the *Inconstant*, little
thinking that we were never to meet again! on this voyage from
which he never recovered.[80] He had the opportunity, however,
before the termination, of shewing that his friendship was sincere
& that his own feelings were as straightforward & as generous as
we believed.

Quebec
Augst 24th
My dearest Mary,
Lambton returned from Montreal the day before yesterday
bringing with him Mr. Duncombe & your letters for which I
thank you exceptionally. There is one thing you say which makes
me feel more grateful than I can express, tho' at the same time it
gives me a little pang of regret. I cannot say how good & kind
I think it was of Papa to have thought of speaking for Lambton
in the H. of Lords about Mr. Turton. I perfectly understand
that not knowing the details of the case between him & the
Govt. it was difficult to say a word, but if he had, what a glorious
thing it would have been! No words can express the happiness I

should have felt at hearing of his speaking in the most trifling case, but in this it would have been most triumphant, & I don't believe the most violent or the most malicious of Lambton's opponents could have said a word more on the subject. I think if Mr. Ellice had chosen, he might have told Papa how good a case Lambton has with Ld. Melbourne & Ld. Glenelg, but I know how disagreeable he is with him upon Politicks, & his son is, I think, much stouter than he is, & I feel much obliged to him for the way he has behaved in this matter. He has had it in his power to be of use, & he has never shrunk from it in the least.

It seems that we have had a great escape in point of heat & fatigue in not going to Montreal Races. Lambton has been very much knocked up by it & many other people have lately had serious attacks, I suppose from over heating themselves. At Montreal the heat seems to have been tremendous, but we had not suffered here at all, & were beginning to find the mornings & evenings very cool, till yesterday when we had a return of as sultry weather as any we have experienced during the summer. This morning the Thermometer is at 80° in the shade. The Admiral is at last gone. He sailed this morning in the Inconstant to our great sorrow. I like him, for himself, of all things, & then he has saved me from so much struggling in being always the person to sit next to me at dinner, that on that account only I should miss him, but he is so kind & good natured to us all, seems so fond of Alice, & takes such pleasure in Mary & Emily's music, that I shall miss & regret him in every way. He is gone straight to Bermuda & as he has had no good accounts of late, I hope he will find his poor daughter much better than when he left her. The two Governors, Sir C. Campbell & Sir C. Fitzroy, also go to morrow. The latter has a very nice boy with him, a little older than George, with whom he has made a great acquaintance, tho' at first they were shy to-gether. Miss Campbell is very delicate—she looks dreadfully ill—& having also been at the Races I have seen less of her, but they say she is better for her trip. The House at Montreal is nearly ready for us. Lambton says it looks very small as it is finished, but there are plenty of rooms & I hope we shall find it comfortable. He has *not yet fixed any time for going there, & as long as the weather continues fine, I think we are better here. I don't understand why so many people give a decided preference for Montreal, in the winter it may deserve it, but for summer I think this has many advantages. Good bye my dearest Mary for to day. I do not yet know when my letter will go. Mary is delighted that her little Toys arrived opportunely for Mary Barrington.*

Saty. 25th

A bag goes this evening so 1000ds of loves & good bye.

Yr. most affect.

Louisa

I wrote to Georgiana by the Hastings *& to you about the same time by New York—also by the* Pique *which was expected to arrive first tho' it sailed a few days later.*

SATURDAY, 25 AUGUST

On the 25th the Governors went. We had liked them both, particularly Sir Colin for his good humour & hearty, friendly manner. They both entered cordially into His views & he was perfectly satisfied in his communications with them. Miss Campbell also gained upon me & Mary after the first impression of rather an affected manner was worn off. She seemed in so miserable a state of health when she came that we felt interested about her, but she appeared much better for her excursion to Canada.

The weather was now decidedly changing, & after a few days we gave up dining early. He continued very unwell for some time after his return & was many days confined to his room. I think he was scarcely out at all before the Races which took place on the Plains of Abraham on the 3rd and 4th of Sept. He was not able to attend them on the first day, but was better and went on the second. He had given a cup & taken pains to encourage them, always promoting these kind of meetings which he thought drew people together in a friendly manner.

Quebec
Sept. 1st

My dearest Mary,

I write to day by the New York Post, but am sorry to say I cannot give you a good account of Lambton. He has never recovered the attack he had at Montreal, & I have not seen him so unwell as he has been within the last few days since the winter at Petersburgh. Of course this disheartens him very much, & I dread very much his prospects for the winter, as the weather is entirely changed & seems as if it was already breaking up. This, altho' perhaps not the first or the only cause of his illness, is at any rate a serious aggravation to it. I have nothing new to tell you. We are waiting with great impatience for later accounts from England, but it must be very uncertain when we may hear again. Mary & I have written by this post to George. We are very sorry not to be at home to see him on his return, & should be very glad if he would come & see us here next spring, as to a Sailor the voyage across the Atlantic is not very formidable. However you would be unwilling to spare him & I suppose he will be glad of a longer rest than that would give him. We must therefore, for every thing, look forward to our return which I hope may take place early in the year. We had an evening party of about 20 Americans the other night. Lambton was not able to appear & I had some struggling. There was among the Ladies a Miss Jones, reckoned a great beauty among all the young gentlemen here & who during the time she staid at Quebec made a great sensation among them, but I am told there is a greater beauty still who is likely to come, I suppose during the Races next week. Pray, my dearest Mary, forgive this very stupid letter & give my best love to Papa & all. I will write again in a few days.

Yr. most affect.
Louisa

I have always forgot to tell you that the bottle for my dressing box arrived quite safe & fits quite well.

We expect Charles & Caroline next week, to stay ten days.

Nothing is yet settled as to the time we go to Montreal. I think
we shall probably remain on here as long as the house is warm
enough with fires without bringing stoves into the rooms.

WEDNESDAY, 5 SEPTEMBER

George's Birthday, a day he always thought much of, had been
fixed for a Regatta. The weather was beautiful, much warmer
than it had been for some days previously, & we found it very
delightful rowing about the river in one of the Men of War
Barges. We met Capt. Crawford⁹¹ sailing in the *Race Horse*. He
went on board & sailed with him a little time, inviting some of
the party, Major & Mrs. Torrens⁹² & Capt. & Mrs. Daniel, to
dinner. These were the English ladies who since our return from
Upper Canada had been living at Quebec, & we had seen them
occasionally of an evening. Mr. & Mrs. Torrens sang a good deal,
& they generally came to help us on the American nights. Mrs.
Daniel also played. Many of the Officers had been away on tours
with their wives but about this time they began to return. We
had now a good deal of rain & cold weather, tho' still many fine
days. On these we drove or sometimes walked in the Chateau
Gardens. There was also a wood beyond the Plains of Abraham
to which we used to go often, getting out to walk there, the children riding. The autumn tints of the foliage were now quite
beautiful & we admired the country more & more. Mr. Duncombe often went with us. We took some long drives to Montmorenci, Lorette, Cap-rouge, but there were still places beyond
we never could reach, such as Lake Charles, Lake Beauport, the
natural steps above Montmorenci &c. The girls rode to one or
two of these with Col. Couper but He never could find time. He
had been better lately but was still often ailing & a good deal
worried by his anxiety for accounts from England. Several things
had passed in Parlt. which were far from satisfactory, & he
became more & more doubtful (with how much reason as it
proved) as to the manner in which the Ordinances of June would
be received & the support which he would obtain from the Govt.
at home.

My dearest Mary,

Lambton is a good deal better than when I wrote last. He was able to go to the last day of the Races & to the Regatta & as the weather happened to be uncommonly fine, he was the better for getting out. Dr Doratt, however, says he has really been very ill, & must expect for a little time to feel some remains of his illness, but I trust he will have no return. The Regatta was a pretty sight, because the day was beautiful & there were a number of gay boats & ships all about, but as to making out much as to what is going on in the matter of the Races, that I must own I never can do. We all went on board the Malabar *which has just been put in great order, having taken in her lower deck guns, & Captain Harvey took us round the Ship to shew us all he had done. Lambton then went on board the* Racehorse, *an* 18 *gun Brig. & sailed about in her for some time. Mary, Emily & I rowed a little while in the Barge & then came on shore as we had as good a view from this house & from the Battery under the windows, as from any other place.*

I have for some time, my dearest Mary, wished to propose to you to number your letters, as by that means I should always know when there is any one missing. I was afraid of asking you to do so before because it sounds formidable, but it seems so very convenient a plan & you are so regular in writing by every opportunity that I am sure you need not be unwilling to adopt it. To set you the example, I have begun myself to day with No. 1, *but I shall not do this with any soul but yourself, for I cannot write often enough to any one else.*

We have been in hopes of receiving Charles & his Wife this week, but their coming has been twice put off & I am beginning almost to fear we shall not see them here at all. Charles had a boat yesterday in one of the Races & it was very near winning but I believe it was badly rowed. He was to have steered if he had been here.

I am hoping for more letters from you & hope when next I hear to find that you are all well & comfortable at Howick. It seems an age since the arrival of the Gt. Western. *There are Newspapers three days later in date by a packet, but of course no letters, tho' I hope soon we may expect some. Pray give my best love to Papa & all & good bye my dearest Mary.*

Yr. *most affect.*
Louisa

Sept. 4th

The post goes to day. I have nothing to add to what I said yesterday but great loves from all.

WEDNESDAY, 12 SEPTEMBER

The *Medea* returned bringing Deputations from among the principal people of Halifax & P. Edward's Island, & on Sunday 16th Charles & Caroline arrived from Montreal.

Quebec
Sept. 13

My dearest Mary,
The Medea *returned yesterday bringing the Halifax Mail which for once was not much behind its time, but which, just this once, has brought no letters for us. I suppose they are coming by New York & in another* 10 *days or so we may expect the* Gt. Western.

I see by the Newspapers that Caroline was in attendance on the Queen so that I trust you are now quite comfortable about dear little Mary, & I hope you may all have been able to get to Howick before the summer was quite over. Here it is at an end, tho' indeed it seems to me to have lasted an immense time—I feel as if we had been six months at least, nearer a year in Canada. We have lately however had very fine weather, tho' with sharp mornings & evenings, but to day we have a storm of wind & rain from the East which blows upon the house with great violence, & has caused us to order the double windows on that side without delay. I am happy to say that Lambton is very much better within the last week. He has found great relief from very small doses of laudanum in those spasmodic pains in the back of his head, but it requires Dr. Doratt's skill to know when to adminis-

ter them properly. He however manages him perfectly & it is the greatest comfort to see that he does understand him thoroughly. The children are all well; Alice in remarkable good looks. We have no letters of any kind but we have seen the account of what passed in Parlt. on Canada affairs after the news of the ordinances. I have not words to express what I think of the wickedness of Ld. Brougham's conduct[93] ⸺ In gratifying his malicious spite he is quite indifferent as to the mischief he may do here. In this I trust he has overacted his part, but that makes no alteration in one's opinion of him.

Lord John seems to have spoken very well & Lambton thinks that Mr. O'Connell[94] has put the question in the right point of view, but he must regret, & so do I very much, that he should have been the person to do it.

Charles & Caroline are not yet come to us. They have been detained waiting for Sir John Colborne who is to inspect the Regiment at Montreal, but I hope they will get here the day after to morrow & remain till the end of the Month.

Pray tell Papa that Miss Campbell (at Halifax) has succeeded in obtaining the promise of a beautiful Labrador Dog, & that in about a month she hopes to be able to send it to England. It will probably be taken to Plymouth & I have desired it may be delivered to the care of Genl. Ellice.[95] I have nothing particular to tell you but pray give my best love to Papa & all—& good bye my dearest Mary.

Yr. most affect.
Louisa

Pray do not forget that I am very likely to want a Maid if you should hear of a good one.

TUESDAY, 18 SEPTEMBER

We drove beyond the Plains of Abraham to observe an Eclipse of the Sun, which we saw perfectly in all its stages.

A day I can never forget! We went a longer drive than usual, crossing a Ferry over a small stream beyond Cap-Rouge, continuing across the country by the St. Fois road. We were a merry party; the children, Charles & Caroline (I think) & Mr. Buller, enjoying the little adventures & difficulties of crossing the Ferry; laughing at Mr. Cavendish & his Drag following us, & delighted with the beauty of the scenery. As we returned we saw from the heights the Steamer from Montreal arriving with the post, tho' little did we guess it, the intelligence of those events whose fatal consequences we were alas! so far from anticipating. We had returned late from our drive & it was time to dress for dinner when we got in. Before I was ready He called me into his room & I could see soon that some thing unusual had occurred. He had received a bag with letters & despatches from England containing the account of the *reception* of the Ordinances, with private letters from Lord Melbourne,[96] Lord Glenelg[97] & others rejoicing over the manner in which the difficult affair of the Prisoners had been settled, & bidding him "go on & prosper," with other expressions of unqualified approbation. There was also a letter from the Queen to me,[98] in answer to those we had written on her Coronation day, expressing her thanks & her satisfaction at all that was going on.

If the Steamer had only brought this bag from England what could have been more gratifying than these communications! But a New York Paper,[99] with later intelligence from home, reversed all these visions of success & happiness. It contained the account of the proceedings of Parlt![100] The disallowance of the Ordinances! &, as it proved, the doom of his fate. I can well remember now the feeling of consternation which came over me on first hearing the news, & indignation & bitter resentment towards those who had so cruelly betrayed Him. He said but little & when he finished his dressing & went with but little delay to dinner, behaving as usual, my heart ached as I looked upon him as he sat opposite me & I thought of the feelings which preyed upon his mind. All the satisfaction that could be afforded by the most lively sympathy & the strongest manifestations of feeling

86

for him, & of indignation against the Govt. & the H. of Lords, He soon received.[101] But the mischief was done. We heard in the course of the evening that the greatest excitement prevailed in town, the news having already spread through it. The most violent language was openly held in the streets; separation from England talked of, & it was said that it would be better to be connected with the United States than with a country which was so reckless of the interests of its Colonies. This kind of feeling was general among all the British Inhabitants of Canada, while on the other hand the French, as soon as they were aroused from their astonishment, became excited and encouraged to resume those intrigues & projects of insurrection, which if never entirely laid aside, had appeared so hopeless that in all probability the attempts to revive them would have been faint & of trifling importance compared with what took place after these events had inspired them with new confidence. Not only among the colonists did such sentiments exist, but in the British Army & Navy, among all the Officers no matter of what party, one general feeling of disapprobation & regret at what had occurred seemed to prevail & the first impression of all, on hearing the news, was that he would not, could not stay; that he must resign & go home instantly. Subsequently these opinions may have been in some measure altered; the country generally was most anxious that he should remain & the greatest alarm was felt about the prospects for the winter, but all his own advisers, & above all Sir John Colborne were most decided in their opinion that his stay was impossible.[102] It had been his own first feeling, but he would have yielded to the wishes of the country, even at the last moment, had Sir John Colborne thought it right to recommend it, but on the contrary he was anxious for his departure.

Within the two first days after the arrival of the news crowds of people came to put down their names at the Govt. House. I believe there was not a respectable person among the British Inhabitants of Quebec who omitted this mark of respect & addresses from all parts of the country soon began to pour in. The most forward in all these demonstrations were the Gentlemen of the Deputations from Halifax, New Brunswick & P. Edward's

Island, & it was in an answer to an address from them that He first publickly made known his determination to resign.

It had been arranged before the news arrived that we were to go on an excursion for two or three days down the St. Lawrence, & perhaps up the Saguenay River, in the *Medea* & every thing was ready to set off the next morning. Even now this project was not entirely given up, tho' He could not be absent so long. We therefore went on board at 8 & ½ but only to go as far as the Falls of St. Anne's which we landed to see. The day was fine, but the morning was cold & for some time it blew very fresh. The landing at St. Anne's was very bad, the steamer could not approach the shore, nor could the Barge get near enough to land us on dry ground. We were obliged therefore to go in carts through the water & across the mud to the shore where we had horses & poney carriages to meet us. There was little water at this season in the cascade, but the rocks are very fine. At another time we should have been much delighted with the beautiful scenery of the mountains & hills on this part of the St. Lawrence, but other feelings were predominant. In order to embark more comfortably on returning, we drove to Chateau Richet, a village at some miles distance where we found the *Medea*. We dined on board & returned home early in the Evening. Mr. Buller, Mr. Duncombe, Charles & Caroline &c. accompanied us on this expedition.

The next day we had a large dinner & went to the Play. His going had been settled some time before at the request of an American Actress, Miss Clifton,[103] but in consequence of the events which had now occurred the House, which in general was very ill attended, was on this occasion excessively full & He was received with the greatest acclaim. The gentlemen of the Deputations dined with us on this & the following day, but after that I think they left Quebec. After the first interviews on arriving they had met him with hearty concurrence in his views for the settlement of the Provinces, & nothing could exceed the interest & friendly feeling which they displayed on the arrival of the news from England. There were among them some very intelligent clever people, very superior in manners & conversation to any we had seen in Canada.

Col. Greville[104] at this time arrived from England. He had come to New York in his yacht & brought letters, but having had a long passage they were all of an old date. He had had no acquaintance with him before & there was nothing which appeared likely to draw them together, but he behaved in a most handsome manner, putting himself & his Yacht at his disposition, offering to return home instantly with Despatches, or to take any person he chose, & seeming anxious to do anything which could be useful or agreeable.

TUESDAY, 25 SEPTEMBER
(In the Evg.) a large mob paraded the streets, & Ld. Brougham was burnt in Effigy.[105]

WEDNESDAY, 26 SEPTEMBER
Letters & Despatches were received from England. It was a beautiful afternoon; we had driven to the Race ground & were walking on the Plains when we saw the Steamer arriving from Montreal. Charles & Mr. Duncombe went down to the Port & He remained with us until they brought the post. The Despatches now contained the official account of what had passed in parlt., but no private letters from the Ministers explaining or attempting to excuse their conduct. Subsequently he had a letter from Lord John Russell admitting that if the circumstances which had occurred had so weakened his authority in the Colony as to render it inefficient for the purposes he had in view on coming out, He was not bound to remain, but would do well to return home. This was the only private communication He received from any one connected with the Govt.

Nothing thus being contained in the Despatches to induce him to make any change in the determination He had already formed, He completed his Despatches in answer, justifying the course he had pursued, & announcing his intention of resigning & returning home,[106] & on Saty. 29th He sent Mr. Cavendish to New York from whence he was to take his passage to England in the *Gt. Western* with these communications. (Charles had left us the night before on some business with his regiment but returned in a week & remained with us till we went.)

We had some beautiful days at this time. On one of them (Friday 28th) we drove below the heights to the Cove. In the villages here there is a considerable population employed in the timber trade, who live quite apart from the town of Quebec, & seem quite a different set of people. The rafts of timber extend a long way into the river, & it is a curious sensation to walk over them. He went to look at some of the shipping & was shewn the manner of loading ships. He met, I believe, with some Vessels from Sunderland. He seemed much interested with this drive. The heat of the sun on this day was very powerful: George having been exposed to it for a long time was affected by it, & was soon after laid up by a severe attack of jaundice.

Quebec
Sept. 28 & 29

My dearest Mary,
I have been in hopes of receiving your letters by the Gt. Western *before the departure of the Messenger who goes by it on its return, but it is not arrived, & he is obliged to set off to morrow. Mr. Cavendish is the bearer of Lambton's resignation, & we shall immediately begin our preparations for departure, so that by the time you receive this we shall probably be actually on our way. You cannot doubt how happy I shall be to see you again so much sooner than we expected, & indeed I am beginning to rejoice altogether at the prospect of being at home, but I have been so distressed at the way in which Lambton has been treated, & at the disappointment & mortification attending the overthrow of all his schemes, that I have hitherto been alive to no other feelings but those of vexation & indignation, & extreme anxiety about his health. I am however at this moment a little easier on that point, & I trust now the crisis is past, that he will reconcile himself to the event & improve in health & spirits. He has however, I assure you, suffered most severely & I have never seen him so reduced in strength. As to the proceedings in the H. of Lords which have produced this change of affairs, I cannot enter upon the subject. I can only say that Lambton has the most trium-*

phant case possible, as I trust all the world will admit, when he is able to bring it out at the meeting of Parlt. Every thing that has taken place here, since the arrival of the news, has been most gratifying & satisfactory to himself, but the change in the prospects of the unhappy country is very dismal & it is grievous to see how all the good which was doing is put a stop to.

It is not yet settled how we go home. The children & I are anxious to see a little bit of the United States & would therefore wish to embark at New York, but there are difficulties about this & it would be easier to go straight from hence in the Malabar, which would soon be ready to take us. I will now my dearest Mary bid you good bye. If I have any thing more to tell you to morrow I will add it to my letter before I put it up. Pray give my best love to Papa & all & good bye my dearest Mary. I have written to none of my sisters, depending upon your telling them of our return.

Your most affect.
Louisa

I received 3 days ago your letters from Howick of the 5th, 6th Augst. There was at the same time news from London up to the 16th. We had heard a week before by an American paper of the proceedings in the Lords.

Lambton says we shall go by the U.S. & be back by the end of the year.

SATURDAY, 29 SEPTEMBER
Mr. Gurney (the Quaker) dined with us; a fine looking man of interesting manners. He was very anxious that He should remain in the country.

TUESDAY, 2 OCTOBER
On another beautiful day, Oct. 2, there was an agricultural meeting near Quebec which He had promised to attend, & to which he went, although He had been ill in bed the day before. We drove to the place & then he rode to look at the different samples of ploughing &c. Separate spots were allotted for the trial of the

French & the English labourers, & it was remarkable to observe the great superiority of the latter. After seeing all that was going on, & getting specimens of straw work &c., we went to the house of a rich old English Farmer who welcomed us with great cordiality. He talked much of his pursuits, & of the difference between the two races; seemed very English in his ideas, but appeared a good speciman of his class.

During the month of October we had many large parties. The arrangements for our departure were proceeding, & many people arrived to see Him before He went. Sir G. Arthur, Genl. Clitherow (accompanied by Mrs. Clitherow), M. Quiblier,[107] from the Catholic College at Montreal &c. We also saw two or three times Mr. Rhet,[108] an American of some note (I believe) in his own country.

FRIDAY, 5 OCTOBER

The *Inconstant* Frigate came in from Bermuda bringing letters from the Admiral, with all the orders that were required for the *Inconstant*, or any other Ship, which might be desired to take us home. The Admiral, tho' still very ill, had been at that moment a little better, & had been able to write himself to L. His letter was what one would have expected; generous, hearty & friendly to the greatest degree, expressing the most lively indignation against the Ministers, & partaking of all the feelings entertained by those around Him who were most attached. It was a letter which did one good. (He sent presents to Alice of Bermuda Straw & two red birds. One of these died on its passage; the other very soon after its arrival at Quebec. We were all pleased at his recollection.)

TUESDAY, 9 OCTOBER

He published, as directed from home, the disallowance of the Ordinances, & the Act of Indemnity, &, at the same time, His own famous Proclamation[109] explaining & justifying His conduct, & giving his reasons for leaving the Colony. This took place at an immense meeting which was held in the Chamber of the H. of Assembly, at which was also presented an address from the

Inhabitants of Quebec signed by 4,287 names. There had never been so large a meeting in Canada; the room was filled to the utmost, & crowds remained outside who were unable to gain an entrance. It was most remarkable too, that those crowds did not consist of the mere rabble, but that the meeting was composed of people of the most respectable appearance, well dressed, and seemingly belonging to the class of tradesmen & shopkeepers. He was received with the greatest enthusiasm, but the excitement in the public mind was such that it seemed to require but little to raise it to violence. His aim was directed to turn their attention towards England, to inspire fresh hopes that his presence & earnest representations, with the faithful report of the state of the country, would at last be met with consideration & produce a change of system in the Govt. of the Colony. This was his object, both in His Speech & answer to the Address, & in the Proclamation which was made the subject of so much reproach in England, & called from the Ministers the formal expression of The Queen's disapprobation. Far, however, from inflaming the minds of the People, the Proclamation had, as was intended the effect of soothing & allaying the irritation & ill feeling which prevailed, by directing their views to the expectation of a last effort in England.

The children & I &c. were present at this meeting, having been given places just behind where he stood. I never beheld any thing like the eagerness with which every word which fell from him seem[ed] to be drunk in. It is to be supposed that He was much affected by the testimonies of respect & confidence which he received on all sides from the People of Canada. He never lost sight of the assurances he gave them of always holding their interests at heart, & using his best endeavours to promote them— & if He took a less prominent part in Parlt., on his return, than his own feelings would have prompted him to do, it was in conformity with the advice of those on whose judgment He had the greatest reliance, & because, on mature reflection, he considered the course He thus pursued, as the most likely to effect the permanent good of the country. But He was ever on the watch, & laboured incessantly till He had completed the *Report*, which amply redeemed his Pledge to the People of Canada. In all this He put *self* out of the question & never suffered his private feelings to interfere where any interest of the Colony was concerned. He gave the Govt. his hearty support, where he thought the advantage of the country required it, not even withholding his approval when the Canada Bill was deferred for another year, altho' by so doing he incurred the animadversions of those who reproached him with receding from the declarations he had made in the *Report* at the beginning of the Session, of the absolute necessity of immediate measures for the settlement of the Country. These measures he had as much at heart as ever, but he thought the Govt., in the circumstances in which it stood after the resignation & return to office of Lord Melbourne,[110] was in no position to carry through the proposed plan, & on so thinking, He considered it most manly to avow his opinion & come forward with his support, altho', on the point of delay, He was not called upon to break the silence He might have preserved with greater appearance of consistency in his own views. Such generosity was worthy of himself, but the Ministers were undeserving of it & incapable of appreciating it, [&] some, even of those who in general were disposed to give him more justice, did not at first understand it. We had hoped that He was to reap the advantages of his forebearance after this first year, & that the representations he might henceforth choose to make, would be listened to with respect & deference. Had He been spared for the Session of '40, He might have taken an active part, but this also was a disappointment He was yet to feel.

Quebec
Oct. 11th

My dearest Mary,
I suppose you receive our letters as we do yours very irregularly as to date—the Gt. Western brought those of the 3rd Sept. but since that we have been going back & have had two arrivals, each older than the other. I had not till to day heard of the spasms from which you had suffered soon after your arrival at Howick, but as the later accounts say you were as well as usual again, I

trust you have had no return. We have been rather uncomfortable since I wrote last about George. He has had a severe attack of jaundice with fever & is yet scarcely out of his room. He is however improving regularly & I hope will have recovered his strength before the 29th, which is the day at present fixed for our Departure. It is settled that we are to go in the Inconstant Frigate which will come for us to New York, or into the Chesapeake, & we shall make a little tour in the United States before we sail. This will be no disadvantage to our passage for they say we are more likely to have smooth weather in December than November, tho' neither of them are reckoned bad months for going home, & if we have any luck we shall be under three weeks on the voyage. How glad I shall be to have a near prospect of seeing you, & yet I rather dread the attacks & discussions which will await Lambton on his return. If I was quite sure he would not mind them, I don't think I should care much, for he has a most triumphant case & every thing that has taken place here is most gratifying. I should feel unhappy at his going, if by remaining he could assist any Mischief to the Country, but it is so clearly the opinion of his friends, & particularly of Col. Couper who is best acquainted with the country, that it is the right course to pursue, that I am at ease on that point, & he will do every thing he can at home for the advantage of the Colony.

Oct. 13th

My dearest Mary,

I have nothing to add, but that George continues to improve & that the Doctor is very positive we need not fear there would be left any remains of his illness. I have been a little uneasy as to the possibility of such a thing, but I hope without reason. Lambton is also much better, he is still overwhelmed with business & is often dreadfully tired, but he has no longer such anxious affairs upon his mind. His proclamation has had the best effect, & is approved of by all parties, even by the French whose discontent had been roused by the proceedings in England. There was an immense meeting to present the address which Lambton received in the Assembly Room. We were present & I never was more *gratified in my life. I could not have believed that Quebec, or any town in this country, could have produced such an assemblage of well dressed, respectable people. They say there were near 3000 people, more than could find room inside the building, altho' that was crowded to the utmost & the feeling displayed most unanimous & enthusiastic.*

All here desire their best love but do not write as we return so soon. Good bye.

My dearest Mary,
I was delighted to hear that Caroline's little girl was so much better for coming to Howick.

Another steamer is due, the Royal William, *but not yet arrived.*

Yr. *most affect.*
Louisa

SATURDAY, 13 OCTOBER
Capt. Conroy[111] was sent home with Despatches.

{To Lord Grey} Quebec
Oct. 13th

My dearest Car,
Lambton is exceptionally busy but he desires me to send you the enclosed paper & also the Gazette with his Proclamation. I trust you will think them satisfactory.[112]

We are all delighted at the prospect of seeing you before long, & indeed we are beginning to rejoice altogether at the thoughts of being at home, tho' for some time I could only think of the disappointment & mortification here. I shall be very glad when our Tour in the States is over, but if we missed this opportunity we should regret it all our lives. We have had a good deal of rain & bad weather lately, but we hope it will be better for our voyage & at any rate we may expect a quick passage.

I hope that George is arrived by this time & quite well. Pray give my best love to him & good bye my dearest Car.

Yr. *most affect.*
Louisa

THURSDAY, 18 OCTOBER

It was decided that we should go straight home to England instead of passing thro' the United States. It had been intended that the *Inconstant* should go round to meet us at New York, & that we should have gone to Washington &c. The accounts however which were now received of the threatening state of the Province[113] induced Him to relinquish this project. He was unwilling, while disturbances & insurrection might be distressing the country to spend any moments in his own gratification, altho' he had considered that his interviews with the President & the leading people of the United States might in other circumstances have done essential service. This might still have been desirable, but other objects seemed now of greater importance, & he was anxious to reach home as soon as possible with the information which He might personally enforce with greater effect. In these views He was strongly encouraged by Sir John Colborne.

(Had he been able to carry into effect his visit to the United States, He would have been received with the greatest honours which had ever been paid to any individual except La Fayette. The preparations were already begun, & Mr. Stevenson,[114] the American Minister communicated to Him officially on his return that He would have been lodged in the *White House* & considered as the Nation's guest).

SATURDAY, 20 OCTOBER

Mr. Dillon[115] went away with Despatches. About this time the Ellice's passed ten days with us. They left on the 28th. Before they went He advised them not to return to Beauharnois.[116]

Quebec
Oct. 20th

My dearest Mary,
This is probably the last letter I shall have an opportunity of writing to you as we are to embark here on the 1st Nov. & to sail directly for England. Lambton has been induced to give up his tour in the United States, as he thinks it right to proceed home with as little delay as possible, in order to lay before the Govt. the critical state of the Provinces. We are all sorry to miss seeing

the United States, or rather (as far as I am concerned at least) to lose the recollections we should have had, but otherwise the journey would have been full of trouble & inconvenience, & it was too late in the year to see the scenery with any advantage, which is the only part of the undertaking which could really have given one pleasure. Edward Ellice has also decided upon returning home by the Gt. Western in December, & tho' one ought to rejoice for Mrs. Ellice, I cannot help feeling very sorry on account of Charles's Wife to whom I think she would have been a great resource in the Winter. However I trust that the 71st will remain at Montreal,[117] & that Charles will not be marched about the country. With so many troops in the Province, I hope there is no danger of any fighting, but the alarm & agitation are so great that it is to be expected there will be constant excitement & harassing reports of all kinds. I was afraid at first that this anxious state of affairs might have made some alteration in Lambton's determination of going home immediately, but his friends agree that he could do no good by staying. Sir John Colborne is strongly of that opinion altho' he decidedly advises that he should not go through the States.

The Inconstant is getting ready as fast as possible. She is supposed to be the fastest sailing Frigate in the Navy, & Capt. Pring[118] talks of the possibility of a voyage of 12 or 14 days. This however is faster than to be wished in point of comfort, but at any rate we are likely to have a favorable wind. We shall probably land at Plymouth.

George has had no return of illness since I wrote. He is still weak & very thin, but he improves gradually, & I hope will soon get on faster. He has been out, but the weather has been rather cold for him. Lambton continues much the same, better perhaps than is to be expected considering the constant business which still grows upon him. The rest are all well & send thousands of loves to you. Good bye my dearest Mary. I cannot express how happy I feel at the thought of seeing you again. My best love to Papa & all.

Yr. most affect.
Louisa

MONDAY, 29 OCTOBER

I went with the girls to see the Ursulines whom we had visited in form so soon after our arrival. They appeared sorry to take leave of us. On this day He went to a Dinner given Him by the Guards who were anxious to shew Him this mark of respect befor He went. Sir James Macdonell, in giving His health, made a speech which was very handsome & very gratifying to Him. This was afterwards found fault with in the H. of Lords by Lord Londonderry.[119] (On this occasion the children & I were alone for the first time—with Caroline.)

TUESDAY, 30 OCTOBER

The next day, Tuesday 30th, He was ill in his room all the morning. We had a large dinner (the last) at which however He was present. There were Sir John Colborne, Sir James Macdonnell &c., & the English ladies in the evening to take leave of us. The parting was quite melancholy. Some of them seemed so anxious & so nervous about their prospects for the winter that I truly felt for them. They all expressed (& I believe sincerely) great regret for our Departure.

WEDNESDAY, 31 OCTOBER

He dined with Sir J. Macdonell at his private house (we were alone with Charles & Caroline). The wind this Evg. was contrary, & we felt uncertain about our Departure which had been fixed for the next day. This was almost sooner than had been intended, but Sir J. Colborne was so anxious He should be gone, & that Military authority alone should prevail in the Province that he remonstrated against all delay. The accounts received now from various quarters were very alarming, & He again proposed at the last moment to remain altogether, but Sir J. Colborne was so decided in his opinion, & expressed so strongly that His presence would only interfere with the exercise of his own military authority, that He could not hesitate in leaving him. But it was unwillingly at last that He did so, as He would have wished to have been at the post of danger.

Another day never to be forgotten.[120] The morning was fine & the wind favorable altho' there was but little of it, & orders were given to prepare for sailing. On the last morning He had yet an opportunity of doing service in the country. The Sheriff from Upper Canada had arrived with unpleasant intelligence of the difficulty of raising the Militia for the Protection of the Province, on account of the little confidence that was felt in the expectation of any effectual exertion on the part of the Govt. at home to obtain the permanent tranquility & welfare of the country. It was supposed that His influence could still be of use, & He had an interview with the Sheriff & the persons who accompanied him, in which He gave them His positive assurances that He believed their interests would be cared for at home, & joined his earnest entreaties that they would look forward once more to a settlement of their difficulties from England, promising that no endeavours should be wanting on His part to further their views. He gave them letters, I believe, to the same effect, & they left Him in better spirits & better hopes as to the success of their exertions.

A little before 2 o'clock all the preparations for embarking were finished, & we set out. We went in procession to the landing place. He was in an open Barouche with me, Sir John Colborne & Sir James Macdonnell. The soldiers were drawn out, & different societies of Quebec (I do not exactly remember what they were) preceded the carriage with Flags, Bands of Music &c.

Crowds of people filled the streets & every position from whence any part of the proceedings of the day could be witnessed. The weather was bright & clear, but intensely cold, the Thermometer on board the *Inconstant* being at 17°. We continued our way down the steep hill & on to the landing place. There was almost a kind of silence prevailing among the dense masses of people who surrounded the carriage. Here & there, at some particular spot, some builder's yard perhaps, acclamations would burst forth, but in general the feelings of deep respect & profound interest seemed to prevent all the common demonstrations of applause, & the gloom which prevailed seemed indeed as if the people were parting with what was most near & dear to them. I never beheld any public ceremony so deeply affecting & all the feelings which pressed upon me on leaving England were slight in comparison of those I now experienced on departing from Quebec. Little did I imagine, on the first occasion, that I could ever feel regret on returning home, but there was now something so sad & so solemn in the scene, so heart breaking in the unmerited disappointment which had befallen upon Him, & upon a great People, that a long life of happiness afterwards could never have effaced the impression made upon me at that moment. [But] what was it then amid the cares & mortifications which followed? The occasion itself was certainly one of the most painful interest, but it has seemed since to have been the foreboding & forerunner of the fatal termination which was impending at so small an interval.

On the deck of the *Inconstant* we took leave of Sir J. Colborne, Sir J. Macdonnell & the gentlemen who had accompanied us on board. Charles & Caroline staid till the last moment, but at last we parted from them also. We saw them afterwards watching us from the Battery of the H. of Assembly (our late home!) as long as they could see us. We were towed out by two steamers, the *Canada* & *Lumber Merchant*, full of people who insisted upon accompanying us until it was dusk. They left us about 6 miles off, at a place called Patrick's Hole, where we anchored for the night. There had been an alarm of Fire in the Ship soon after we first came on board. He was told of it by Capt. Pring, but it was happily extinguished & we did not know of it until all the anxiety was over.

I seem to have been speaking principally of myself—of my own sensations—but it was the sight of Him, of His countenance, which contributed to render them so intense. He said but little at the moment & soon the incidents of the voyage occupied his immediate attention.

We returned in the *Inconstant* a very small party in comparison with that which we had come out in the *Hastings*. It now consisted of the two Aide de Camps who remained (Mr. Villiers & Mr. Ponsonby), Sir J. Doratt & Mr. Duncombe. The ship was made very comfortable, & arranged in the best way for so long a voyage at so unfavorable a season of the year. The cabins, by Capt. Pring's advice, were made very tight & very secure, & altho' they appeared dark & close at first, we found the advantages of the arrangements in the bad weather we had to encounter. The After Cabin was light & airy when we could have the windows open, but it was necessary to keep up the dead lights during the greater part of the voyage. We were again most fortunate in our Captain. Nothing could exceed Capt. Pring's kindness & attention, & his care for our comfort & activity were unwearied.

FRIDAY, 2 NOVEMBER

On Friday 2nd there was little wind & we anchored in the Evg. before we reached the Brandy Pots, the *Andromache*, which was also leaving the St. Lawrence, having joined us. The cold on this day was excessive. He came to dinner, but soon after was seized with a violent attack of Fever—perhaps the consequence of a chill He may have taken on embarking the day before, or of the change from the warm rooms He had been used to on shore. However it was, He was very ill, & Capt. Pring hung up his cot in the After Cabin that He might be more comfortable & have the benefit of the stove. I remained with him all that night. Next day He was somewhat better but continued in bed all day.

SATURDAY, 3 NOVEMBER

On that morning the Ship touched ground, & there was an alarm of a leak. We anchored to ascertain the fact but it was found that no mischief had been done. On first hearing of this accident He was inclined to suspect (so many of the Queen's Ships having already been on shore) that the French Canadian Pilot had intended to lead us into a scrape, but it did not appear to Capt. Pring, or those who were able to investigate his conduct, that he was in any way to blame.

SUNDAY, 4 NOVEMBER

He was rather better. For the first 3 or 4 days our passage was quite smooth. The cold was excessive but the wind was moderate

& favorable & being still under the shelter of the land we had scarcely any motion in the Ship. This enabled Him to have his cot in the After Cabin while he was so very ill & while the cold was so severe.

MONDAY, 5 NOVEMBER
We were becalmed with a fog & Capt. Baynes[121] from the *Andromache* came on board to dinner. On this night it began to blow very hard and next day, Tuesday 6th, the wind was up against us with a very heavy swell. From this time we had scarcely any intermission of rough weather for the whole of the passage—not an entire day's fair wind—& a succession of gales, some of them very heavy.

THURSDAY, 9 NOVEMBER
We were quite out of the gulf. This day was fine with a gentle wind & we enjoyed a little rest. He now returned to his own cabin, having found great inconvenience from the motion in the other. The ship rolled very much when there was any wind & there was a great deal of trouble in securing things in the After Cabins. We did not however suffer from the cold after we were out of the gulf, so that He did not find the want of the stove in his removal. The attack of Fever, which had been very severe after He first embarked, was not long in yielding to the remedies which were employed, & we hoped He was getting well, but having been imprudently allowed to go out on deck too soon, he caught a cold in his face & suffered a great deal from that, & his usual attacks in the head, for the remainder of the voyage. He was constantly confined to his Cot.

SUNDAY, 11 NOVEMBER
We were on the Banks of Newfoundland. It was blowing very hard & every preparation was made for bad weather. [On] the 12th & 13th the gale was very heavy.. We were under first storm staysails & then obliged to lay to. The 14th it still continued, but abating a little in the course of the day, we made sail again. I believe this was the first gale we had. On one occasion the only sail

we had up to steady the Ship was split in pieces with a noise like thunder, & at another time one of the guns on the fore part of the ship was forced out of place, an immense bolt having been bent round with extraordinary violence. We continued after this to have a great deal of bad weather; heavy squalls, swell & terrible rolling of the ship, but occasionally finer intervals, & when it was possible we passed some time on deck.

SUNDAY, 18 NOVEMBER

Having been better for the last day or two He was on deck & came to dinner, & I think from this time He continued to improve. George also, who had but just recovered from his illness when he set out, regained his strength very fast.

We became, as may be imagined, terribly weary of this tedious & boisterous passage. On one day, when it was blowing very hard, we might have made the coast of Ireland, & most of us would have been much rejoiced to have done so, but it would have disturbed the Captain a good deal. We continued our course & on Sunday 26th, were in sight of St. Agnes Light house, on one of the Scilly Isles, about 10 o'clock in the morning, & of the Eddystone about 10 P. M. The wind had been fine this day, & as we approached at night, we pressed all sail not to lose it, as it appeared to be changing a little. The night was fine & very mild, but rather dark, & as we remained on deck it was pretty to watch the Ship cutting her way through the water. We passed a Steamer very close, & went close under some of the high rocks at the entrance as we took our station & anchored within the Breakwater. The noise of the anchor dropping was a joyful sound to us all. We fancied now that all our miseries were at an end, & that no bad weather now could signify to us. As soon as a boat could be lowered Mr. Ponsonby was sent on shore with a Midshipman to announce our arrival & enquire for any letters that might be waiting for us. Not an hour afterwards the wind rose & soon encreased to a heavy gale. The boat was not able to return, & next morning we found that there was no hope of being able to land while it blew with such violence. We had a letter in the morning from Genl. Ellice, brought (I think) by the Harbour

Master, who was going round to look after Ships in distress, but no boats could stay out. In the afternoon the wind was more moderate & the Admiral sent his Yacht alongside in case we were able to come on shore, but there was still so much sea that Capt. Pring would not recommend our leaving the ship, fearing we would get very wet. Mr Villiers, however, was put on board & was desired to take a message to the Admiral begging he would send back again, as should the wind continue to fall it was probable we might be able to land a few hours later. This was indeed the case. The evening was quite fine & calm but the Admiral would not send back the Yacht, & it was not thought adviseable to land in the boats. At night it began to blow again, & the whole of Wedy. & Thursday we had a tremendous gale. The Ship was riding at a great length of chain, extremely uneasy. We were obliged to have every thing secured in the cabins as if we had been at Sea, & her position appeared very frightful. Enormous waves dashed over the Breakwater, & a French Brig came in, in the utmost distress, nearly dismasted, her colours reversed & her crew clinging to the rigging. He & the girls were on deck at the time. For some moments it appeared as if nothing could save her striking on the Breakwater, but she just escaped it & got in. Several Ships were damaged & we heard afterwards that the crew of a boat (2 or 3 men) were lost in endeavouring to get out to the *Inconstant*. Next morning, Friday 30th, the wind abated; we landed in the *Inconstant*'s Barge & went to Gov't. House, where we found Eliza & Bess,[122] who had been watching for us with great anxiety from the time we arrived within the Breakwater.

SATURDAY, I DECEMBER
An address was presented to him in the Town Hall. The weather was most unfavorable; it rained incessantly, but the Hall was crowded to the utmost, & He was received & listened to with the greatest enthusiasm. We remained at Devonport with General & Mrs. Ellice till Tuesday 4th. All this time He received no communications from the Ministers, or any of his friends, but exaggerated reports reached him of the hostility which prevailed

against him on the part of the Gov't., the Queen &c. The people did not share in such sentiments but received him every where with the greatest cordiality, & on his way to town addresses were presented to him at Ashburton, Exeter & Honiton. On Tuesday 4th we dined & slept with Lord & Lady Morley at Saltram; set off early next morning & reached London on Friday 7th.

On his arrival in town He received Duplicates of the Despatches which had been sent to Canada but had reached Him before his Departure, containing the official disapprobation of the Govt. & the Queen to the Proclamation &c. & unaccompanied by one private line expressing regret at what had occurred. The consequence was the cessation of all intercourse with the Ministers in private, tho' he still offered to afford any communication which might be of service to the Public, & prepared to arrange his *Report* on his Mission. On the 10th (I think) He sent in the last formal resignation of his appointment, which had not yet been delivered, & at the same time my resignation of the place of Lady of the Bedchamber. The feelings of disappointment & mortification which pressed on Him at this time were very acute. There appeared great backwardness on the part of many from whom He might have expected more cordiality, while on the contrary, others on whom He had no claim came forward most unexpectedly. Lord Hill[123] was among the first to call upon Him. This He considered as a civility on acknowledgement of the attention He had shewn the Officers of the Army in Canada. But it was Sir Willoughby Gordon whose conduct was that of a sincere & honest friend. He lost not a moment in coming to him; gave all his attention to the circumstances of His case, & by his judgement & advice was of great use in confirming & encouraging Him in that course of moderation & forebearance which he soon determined upon pursuing. His own feeling of resentment for Canada, and for Himself, might naturally have led Him at first into a more violent line of conduct, & the Radical leaders would gladly have hailed him as their chief, but He resisted all such temptations & stood resolutely aloof as best befitting his own dignity & the position He held in the world. This conduct brought round many who at first had been inclined to hang back.

His report was ready & printed by the meeting of Parlt.[124] There was a delay of a few days in publishing it on the part of the Govt., of which he asked the reason on the day of the meeting, but it soon appeared, & the approbation of the Queen was conveyed to Him by Lord Glenelg (his last act before leaving office.)[125] On the first days of the session some trifling attacks were made upon Him by some of the Tory Peers; (I think) Ld. Wharncliffe,[126] Ld. Wicklowe[127] & Ld. Winchelsea,[128] who revived the affair of Mr. Turton, but they were completely silenced by his answers, & the Govt. brought no charges against him. The Session thus passed on with the tranquillity which was little to have been expected from the appearance of affairs when we returned home. Angry feelings by degrees subsided; he met several of the Ministers in private, & when towards the end of the session He came up from Cowes to attend the Canada Debate[129] in the H. of Lords, they were happy to get his support. He gave it to them most generously, even expressing his consent to delay, altho' at the beginning of the year He had strongly urged the necessity of immediate measures for the settlement of the Provinces. Seeing, however, that in the present state of parties no good was likely to be done, He thought it more manly & more likely to promote the permanent advantage of the Colony; to give his approbation openly & decidedly to the proposed delay. He was attacked for this in some of the Liberal papers, but most unjustly, as I believe they afterwards admitted. Also when Mr. Poulett Thomson was appointed to Canada, He afforded him all the information & assistance it was in his power to bestow. He met him in London the beginning of Sept. & afterwards, when he came down to Portsmouth, He went over from Cowes to him & remained to see him off in the *Pique*. Mr. Poulett Thomson's[130] family afterwards expressed their gratitude for all He had done on this occasion.

He was not able to take part in the Session of '40, but He saw the triumph of His views for Canada, & could foresee the success of His principles. Justice is as yet but imperfectly done to Him, at least in England, but the time may come when He will be better appreciated.

My dearest Mary,

I have been some days without writing but having sent you one line on our landing & knowing that you had heard from Bess I have indulged myself in idleness. Besides I felt that sort of suspense about every thing that I have no heart to write even to you. I had been full of anxiety about our own concerns, but at this moment I am so shocked at the idea of what has been passing in Canada that all other feelings are deadened. I trust we shall in a few days have much later intelligence by the Gt. Western & *that we may hear something satisfactory about the Ellices.*[131] *Lambton does not think there is cause for alarm as to their actual safety, but it is frightful to think of the alarm & distress poor Mrs. Ellice must have endured. I am angry too, for Edward Ellice should not have taken her back to Beauharnois. He was advised over & over again not to do so, but his Father had desired him to remain & finish some business & he was obstinate. His Father must now be very miserable. You will also be very anxious about Charles & in this feeling you may think we all share most deeply.*

We are all well but the weather has been so bad that we have not yet been able to get our things from the Inconstant. *We expect however now to be able to set off on Wednesday. We go to Saltram to dine & sleep to morrow. Bess went to day. My best love to all & good bye my dearest Mary.*

Yr. most affect.
Louisa

Saturday

My dearest Mary,

I have this day again received letters from you which have followed us back from Canada. In every one there are proofs of your great affection & kindness to me. Of this indeed I have always been fully convinced & I only feel that I never can make a sufficient return, tho' I do love you with my whole heart & soul.

Of course you have heard from Charles. Lambton has a letter from him & I was glad to find that he does not speak as if Caroline was coming to Beauharnois.[132] *She is very sensible to cold, & I am very sure she could not be comfortable in Mr. Ellice's house, even as we saw it, & I hope he will soon get to her at Montreal. He says he has made his house there very comfortable. I dare say Charles has told you the same, that he is rejoiced Lambton came away, & that every thing which happens proves more & more the misfortune of having interfered with the ordinances. He says it is very lucky Lambton had not to take the measures Sir J. Colborne has been obliged to have recourse to, as he would not have been supported at home.*[133] *I am most sincerely grieved at the state of the country, but I must own that it is a satisfaction to see how right Lambton's policy has proved. I suppose that they will not interfere with Sir J. Colborne, & for the present moment he is the best person they could have there, but people say he is, & feels himself, unequal to civil affairs.*

Thousands of loves my dearest Mary to Papa & all & good bye.

Yr. most affect.
Louisa

Monday, Decr. 9, '38

My dearest Mary,
I meant to have written to you to day but have been prevented till the last moment before the post.

I have sent my resignation to the Queen. We did not come home intending to take this step & Lambton was prepared to be of what use he could, & to give to the Ministers any information they required, but having received the Despatch which was sent out to him expressing the Queen's disapprobation, *& no other communication from them of any kind since he arrived, there is but this course to pursue.*

I shall write again to morrow or soon but must now bid you good bye with my best love to Papa & all.

Yr. most affect.
Louisa

My dearest Mary,
I suppose you have by this time received accounts of Charles by the Gt. Western. *We had a long letter from Caroline who was only uneasy then about us, on account of an exaggerated story of the* Inconstant's *touching the ground, & being so damaged that she was obliged to go to Halifax. Lambton thinks the danger in Lower Canada over, but I am not so sure that he is quite so easy about the Upper Province where the people to be feared are of a very different kind from the French Canadians. However he thinks the President's Proclamation very good, & I hope it will be useful. He had a long letter from Sir G. Arthur, & among other things he told him that he had lately seen a respectable Merchant from the United States, who had been living near where some of the Refugees[134] were settled, & from him he had had an account of the joy that was expressed among them when the news arrived of the disallowance of the Ordinances. They considered it a complete triumph, & there is no doubt that from that moment they carried on their plans with renewed spirit & activity.*

I should think the Ellices might be expected any day.[135] They were to have sailed from New York the 20th or 24th Novr. & probably they would not be more inclined to delay after their adventures. Of these we have heard a woeful account, but they seem not to have been the worse when all was over. All the passages since ours have been uncommonly quick. Col. Couper is arrived in England, & Mr. Buller & the rest must soon follow. I cannot tell you how I long to have every thing known that has taken place with respect to Lambton. The private letters from Ld. Melbourne & Ld. Glenelg approving of the ordinances can never appear,[136] but I think enough must come out to make his case very triumphant, & I am only unhappy that the meeting of Parlt. is deferred, because it is keeping him so long in a state of worry, & also confining him & the children to this nasty town. We have however no recourse. We can think of no place near London to go to, & as he is advised to be as quiet as possible, which I feel sure Papa would think right, the North, where there would be meetings & addresses without end, is quite out of the question.

I have forgot since I came to tell you a piece of news of a different sort, which I think will surprise you as much as it did me. Sophie is married! to a tailor "très honnête homme" at Paris. I found a letter from her announcing the event, & telling me that she had taken the step as much for my sake as for her own, for that she felt she was not able to take long journies or to work, as her sight was failing & that had she to leave me for a 2nd time, the 2nd separation would be as bad as the first. However she does not otherwise complain of her health, & I hope she is happy & comfortable.

I am longing to see Caroline. I hope little Mary will arrive quite well. I think Charlie is looking wonderfully stronger & better than he used to. He dined on Sunday with our children. Good bye my dearest Mary. Pray give my best love to Papa & Georgiana & George.

Yr. most affect.
Louisa

APPENDIX

SKETCH OF LORD DURHAM'S MISSION
TO CANADA

CHARLES BULLER[137]

A complete history of Lord Durham's mission to Canada would be a work requiring much research respecting a long chain of preceding and a great variety of contemporaneous events. Nor is the time yet come for giving such a history with the minuteness and accuracy which I should desire. Time must yet elapse before we shall be able sufficiently to develop much of the secret motives and acts of the parties concerned. Nor are the general bearings and results of what then occurred become yet sufficiently apparent for the world in general to appreciate in their full extent the magnitude and usefulness of the measures then adopted. It is still matter of interest, of pique, or of a false point of honour with great parties and powerful individuals to refuse to the memory of Lord Durham that justice which could not be granted without condemning their conduct, or stripping them of the credit which they wish most unjustly to arrogate to themselves. We, whose first purpose must be to secure him justice, have however but to wait till time shall attain for us the object which we have at heart. True and lasting fame must almost always be earned as much by patience as by merit. And sure may we be that if our estimate of Lord Durham's policy and acts during this mission be correct, the results will unfold themselves in such a manner as to force even the most inattentive or prejudiced to view them aright. The interests, and the passions too, that have hitherto thwarted our endeavours to obtain justice will in the same manner be dispelled by mere lapse of time; and it will probably not be long ere some of the very parties and individuals that have hitherto fancied it their interest to decry Lord Durham will find policy as well as justice inducing them to vindicate for him the honour which others seem inclined to usurp. My purpose in writing this sketch of the mission to Canada is to give a succinct view of the state of affairs with which Lord Durham had to deal; of the incidents which occurred during his government; of the steps that he took in order to overcome the immediate difficulties which he had to encounter; and of the plans, by which he purposed to put the government of the North American Colonies on a footing of permanent tranquillity, freedom, and progress.

My personal acquaintance with Lord Durham only commenced in the summer of 1837, on his return from Russia; and I had seen very little of him at the time when the Bill for the temporary government of Canada was brought into Parliament. Absolute as the necessity of some such measure was, it would have been very difficult to get the assent of all parties to the establishment of such a power in the hands of any other individual than Lord Durham. So high did he stand in the estimation of all parties that the Tories were obliged to be as unanimous in their acquiescence as the Liberals of every shade were in their loud approval. His memorable speech in the House of Lords on the night that the measure was first announced in it, increased the feeling of confidence in him. Such an occasion admitted indeed of no display of reasoning or information; but Lord Durham's short speech showed that he was actuated by a firm determination and a spirit of most impartial justice; it marked a deep sense of the heavy responsibility which he had taken on himself; and it breathed a chivalrous reliance on the cordial support of friends, and the generous forbearance of opponents, that made both of them affect a show of such feelings and led the public to believe that they entertained them. This was most unfortunate for Lord Durham, for it led him to expect cordial support and generous forbearance where prudence would have induced to count on one as little as the other, and thus have spared him the pain of the double disappointment which he afterwards experienced.

It was a day or two after this speech that Lord Durham, while sitting under the gallery of the House of Commons, desired me to call on him the next morning. Anticipating the purpose for which he desired to see me, and having had a good deal of discussion on the subject with my own family, I went to the interview having made up my mind not to accept of any offer of going out to Canada. Lord Durham made me the proposal in very flattering terms, and with much kindness. I was not very easily induced to change my resolution, but he desired me to take a little time for consideration ere I gave my final answer; and the result of reconsideration and of consultation with friends was that the next morning I accepted the offer.

I wish that it had so happened that at the period of my thus undertaking to serve under Lord Durham our acquaintance had been of longer standing, and that I had been on those terms of perfect confidence with him to which I very soon attained. For though nothing could be more uniformly kind than Lord Durham was to me from the first, tho' he was not long in giving me his confidence, and when he gave it, gave it as he always did, without reserve, yet the mere awkwardness arising from imperfect personal acquaintance is enough in any case for some time to prevent a sufficiently free communication between two people. Had we at the outset been on the terms on which we got in a very few weeks, I think I might have enabled Lord Durham to avoid what always struck me at the time and has, I think, since proved to have been an error most injurious to the success of the mission. This was the delay that occurred before we entered upon it; and though the season of the year placed some difficulties in the way of our going to Quebec in the mode that appeared most desirable, I think that Lord Durham's first object should have been that of commencing his work with promptitude. The delay took off the bloom of the Mission; the insurrection was to all appearance wholly suppressed before we started; the danger began to be thought less urgent; and the general impression of the necessity for great powers and unusual measures was gradually weakened. We soon felt the effect of this, for as the first alarm so the first unanimity wore off, and the Tories, as they recovered spirits, began to find all manner of faults with the Mission, and to circulate a variety of falsehoods, to draw invidious comparisons between Lord Durham and Sir John Colborne, and to depreciate the moral effect of the powers of the new Governor-General.

This altered state of feeling soon began to show itself in the Press, and in Parliament we had a very unpleasant indication of it in the very near success of Lord Chandos's motion respecting the expenses of the Mission. Soon after that difficulties began to be experienced with respect to the appointment of Mr. Turton; and the opposition to Lord Durham here commenced on the part of supporters and members of the Government. It is impossible now not to regret an appointment, which was the occasion of so much subsequent annoyance and evil. Useful as Mr. Turton's legal knowledge and abilities were, and creditable to Lord Durham as was his eagerness to avail himself of the opportunity afforded him of serving an old and unfortunate friend by the suggestion of giving him the appointment, which was made to him by Mr. Stanley, and urged on him by Sir John Hobhouse, yet it cannot but be regretted that the appointment was ever made, and still more so that after the difficulties, which prevented its being sanctioned by the Colonial Office, Mr. Turton should have been taken out without the written approval of the Ministers. But there was the very clearest understanding respecting the terms on which Mr. Turton was to go out. It was distinctly arranged between them and Lord Durham that though the appointment was not to be made by Ministers or in England, Mr. Turton was to go out with us, it being left to Lord Durham to appoint him to office on his own responsibility after our arrival in Canada. Lord Durham, confiding in the promised forbearance of the Tories and the cordial support of the Ministers, left the matter on this footing of clear but unwritten understanding. Unhappily we had none of us then learned how necessary it was to distrust both.

It is painful now to recall the circumstances of our embarkation in the *Hastings*. I had got on board about an hour before Lord Durham came, and, having found everything in my cabin in utter confusion, I had been exerting myself so busily in seeing things arranged as well as possible that every melancholy thought naturally excited by leaving England had been for the moment completely put out of my mind. I had just got over my difficulties, when the steamer bringing Lord Durham and his family came alongside. All the parade of naval reception was of course exhibited on the occasion; the marines were drawn up, and the Officers, with the captain at their head, were on the deck, when Lord Durham, who had been very ill the night before, came looking very pale, and wrapped up in a large cloak, with Lady Durham and his children around him. Painful thoughts arose within me at the sight of a man so distinguished leaving his country with his whole family for what, though an honourable, was still a painful exile, and a duty of arduous responsibility; and when on a sudden the band struck up its loud and slow strain, the sudden excitement brought the tears at once into my eyes. I did not long indulge these feelings, I thought that this was but a passing and necessary trial attendant on the outset of a career of high utility and honor, of which the first glory would be the pacification of Canada, and the ultimate reward would be re-nown, power, and happiness at home. But the foreboding of the first moment was unfortunately more prophetic than my calmer afterthought!

In one respect we did most certainly merit success: for never I believe, did men embark in any public undertaking with more singleness and honesty of purpose. During the long period of our voyage out we read over all the public documents connected with the subject of our Mission, and the Dispatches, Instructions, and other papers with which the Colonial Office had supplied us; and very fully did we discuss all the various and difficult questions which it appeared to us that we should have to solve. We had, I must again say, very little thought of ourselves, and a very absorbing desire so to perform our task as to promote the best interests both of Canada and of Great Britain. And I think I may also say that we had very few prejudices to mislead us. I used indeed then to think that Lord Durham had too strong a feeling against the French Canadians on account of their recent insurrection. I looked on that insurrection as having been pro-voked by the long injustice, and invited by the deplorable imbecility of our Colonial policy; and I thought that our real sympathies ought to be with a people whose ultimate purposes were right, though by the misconduct of others they had been driven into rebellion. But Lord Durham from the first took a far sounder view of the matter: he saw what narrow and mischievous spirit lurked at the bottom of all the acts of the French Canadians; and while he was prepared to do the individuals full justice, and justice with mercy, he had made up his mind that no quarter should be shewn to the absurd pretensions of race, and that he must throw himself on the support of the British feelings, and aim at making Canada thoroughly British. . . .

In spite, however, of all our occupations we got somewhat tired of our voyage before the first land on the American Continent met our eyes. An ungenial aspect did our new home present to us as we lay for two or three days beating about at the mouth of the St. Lawrence, now looking at the long low desert island of Anticosti, now borne close to the unpeopled forests of Gaspé, and now catching a glimpse of the icy rocks of Labrador glittering in the far distance. Here, however, we received a file of Quebec papers, that gave us some insight into what was passing in Lower Canada. Nor was the information by any means assuring. The French Canadians, it is true, appeared to be making no movement; but for this very reason it seemed to be generally apprehended that they were preparing their forces for some new attempt. The people of the United States were represented as universally fomenting and aiding the designs of the disaffected, and as hardly to be restrained from breaking out into open hostility. Amid all these dangers the British population of Lower Canada was evidently torn in pieces by numerous and furious dissensions. A very violent party, while it called for war with the United States, and for the harshest measures against the French Canadians, kept no terms with its own government, and denounced both Local and Imperial authorities in the most unmeasured terms. We learned that a few days before, in anticipation of our arrival, a meeting of the British population had taken place at Quebec. At this the violent party appeared to have carried the day; various speakers had used language expressive of very little confidence in the Governor-General, and an address had been adopted which, though it contained nothing positively offensive, showed the bad spirit that animated those who had assumed the lead of what was called the British party. This intelligence, disagreeable as it was, proved nevertheless of use, because it prepared Lord Durham beforehand for the kind of feeling and language which he was to meet with on landing. And during the two or three days that elapsed before our arrival at Quebec he prepared the proclamation to the Inhabitants of British North America which he published on disembarking. . . .

Our landing did not take place for a couple of days, but from the moment of our arrival in the harbour we received the visits of the various authorities and public Officers of the Province.

At the very moment of landing, and taking upon himself the government, it became necessary for Lord Durham to resolve upon a very important and bold step. For it was usual for the new Governor immediately after having taken the Oaths of Office, to proceed to swear in those of whom he intended to form his Executive Council, and the custom had been for every new Governor to continue the Council of his predecessor. This, however, Lord Durham had made up his mind not to do, and subsequent reflection has only more and more convinced me that this was the wisest course of conduct which he could have pursued. The strange system of colonial government, by which every person once in office was held in practice to be for ever irremovable, had had the effect of filling the Executive Council with some of the oldest men of every clique that had in succession ruled the Province. Many of these either happened to have been subordinate members of their party, or to have been selected simply because they were attached to no party, and being men of little strength of character, or position in public life, were likely to be very docile agents of the one or two persons who really managed the government. No one of them possessed the confidence of the British population. . . . All the component parts of the Executive Council were in truth generally obnoxious and destitute of moral influence. Lord Durham did quite wisely in keeping clear of them, and in letting the public see that he did so. He resolved at once not to retain the Executive Council, but to form a new one, which might discharge the mere acts of routine to which the Constitutional Act required the assent of an Executive Council, composing it of persons who had either come with him from England, or who had previously taken little part in the politics of the Province. Accordingly he determined at the outset to compose his Council of his three Secretaries, together with the Commissary General, and Mr. Daly, the Provincial Secretary, whom Sir John Colborne had recommended as the most unexceptionable of the public officers of the province. This determination shocked the prejudices of the old official body, and not only was it the subject of warm remonstrances beforehand, but on the occasion of the investiture, the Clerk of the Council, though apprised of Lord Durham's intention, attempted to surprise him into swearing in the whole Council as a matter of course. But this attempt Lord Durham checked very decisively, and the same day he put into my hands the draft of a letter, in which I was to inform the Executive Councillors of his determination, and of the grounds on which he had formed it. This document was taken as the programme of a new system of administering the government free of the influence of these local cabals, which were odious to the whole province. The act of dispensing with the old Executive Council, and the statement of the grounds on which it was done, were not unpalatable to the British, and very gratifying to the French Canadians. "Il a fait déjà une bonne chose," said an old inhabitant at Montreal to Mr. Viger, who asked him what he thought of the Governor-General; "it a tué les deux Conseils."

This measure has, however, been blamed as if Lord Durham had thereby voluntarily deprived himself of the valuable advice of all the persons best acquainted with the mysteries of provincial government, and of the moral influence of their character and experience. The value of their individual advice and influence I have already shown. It must not be supposed, however, that Lord Durham was insensible to the necessity of local experience and wise advisers. But the truth was that from its official ranks the province could supply him with no advisers on whom he could safely rely. With the exception of Mr. Daly, every one of the body had been so mixed up with the ancient and odious system of exclusive government and jobbing—had rendered himself so obnoxious to one party or the other, or more often to all—and had contracted such violent antipathies, that it would have been most imprudent to trust to their representations and advice. We found the whole machine of government utterly disorganized and powerless. The Official body, as the head of whom we might still regard Mr. Sewell, the Chief Justice of the province, was a class perfectly apart from every other, possessing the confidence neither of French nor of British, and exercising not the slightest influence over the public mind. The Chief Justice had for some years ceased to play an important part in politics, and at the period of our arrival his age had wholly unfitted him for active exertions. Of the younger members of the official body none had at all exhibited talents so remarkable as his, or could be relied upon as an impartial or capable adviser of the Government. The Attorney-General, Mr. Ogden, whose office was really the most important in the Province, though a much more kindly disposed and honest man than my previous notions had led me to expect that I should find him, was, after all, endowed with so little political knowledge or capacity that it was impossible for Lord Durham to place any reliance in his advice. Our official advisers were, in fact, men of little capacity and great unpopularity. Lord Durham could have gained little from their counsels except the contagion of their party antipathies and the odium of being supposed to be under their influence.

When we came to look around us, and endeavoured to judge of the feelings and situation of the different classes of the population, it appeared at first sight utterly impossible to ascertain the truth about either. The great mass of the population of Lower Canada—those of the French race—appeared to be placed utterly beyond the reach of any communication with the Government. There could, however, be no doubt that this whole population was thoroughly disaffected to the British Government; that it remained brooding over the memory of its late defeat and the annihilation of its recent predominance; and that it cherished the hope of avenging its imagined wrongs and triumphing over its rulers by means of more combined insurrection and the aid of foreign arms. The greater part of its ancient leaders were fugitives or prisoners; of the few who remained in Canada some were too timid, some too full of resentment, to take any open part in politics; and some, whom we had imagined to possess great influence, appeared to have become objects of suspicion to their countrymen. The Catholic clergy in the diocese of Quebec, under a good and quiet bishop, were loyal and well disposed; those of the diocese of Montreal, under the influence of their bishop, Lartique, were supposed in many instances not to be very well affected. But the priesthood had in great measure lost their influence, and though we made use of them at first as a means of formal communication with their parishioners, and though they sometimes gave us useful private information, they supplied us with no channel of efficient intercourse with the French. With the mass of that body the Government could, in fact, get into no confidential communication. Their desires, as far as they could be ascertained, seemed to be wild and impracticable. All demanded, and perhaps the greater part really expected, that the new Government would attempt to conciliate them by placing things just in the position in which they had been before the insurrection, that Lord Durham would re-establish the Constitution which Parliament had suspended, bring back the Local Assembly with its French majority, grant a complete amnesty to the insurgent leaders, and trust them with all the powers that they had been used to demand during the period of their greatest influence and most exaggerated pretensions. Some hopes of a more reasonable kind, a few of the leaders of the party appear to have entertained from the known liberal views of Lord Durham. But the language of their addresses was constrained and cold; in some cases it was such that Lord Durham felt compelled to check their extravagant demands, and the great body of them immediately relapsed into their sullen and distant apathy.

The leaders of the British party, who were for the most part leading merchants in Montreal, with one or two of the same class in Quebec, were the men who had for some time, through their influence in the Legislative, and subsequently in Sir John Colborne's Special Council, exercised a great influence over the Government of the Province, and were little pleased at the change of circumstances, which partly by the necessary consequences of the suspension of the Constitution, and partly by Lord Durham's own policy, had excluded them from all direct share in the Government. These men, however, had too much tact voluntarily to place themselves in open collision with the Governor-General. The mass of the British population, however, heated by the fierce conflict of the two races, were after all in the main actuated by very laudable purposes. Their main object was the tranquillity and improvement of the Province, whereby they hoped that their own industrial occupations might be rendered more secure and profitable.

The subversion of the French ascendancy had gone far to satisfy most of them and the appointment of Lord Durham to exercise the vast powers vested in the Governor-General had been popular with the great mass of them, because from his liberal opinions and known energy of character they expected that speedy and extensive reforms would be made in the obnoxious institutions of the Province, and a great impulse given to its internal improvement. The leaders, seeing this tendency among them, had gone with them in it: the cold and repulsive spirit of the meeting at Quebec had found very few imitators in the Province; the addresses of the British were general and warm, and the deputations that presented them were numerous and friendly, and Lord Durham improved their good dispositions by the reception which he gave them. All his answers to their addresses shewed how skilfully he had divined the true mode of acquiring their confidence. He appealed boldly and strongly to the feelings which he knew to animate the British population. He spoke always of the greatness of the Mother Country and of the importance and wonderful capabilities of the colony, and, appealing to them to use every effort to improve its resources, promised them an efficient co-operation on his own part and that of the Imperial Government. By these means he speedily excited among them an enthusiasm and attachment such as no Governor before or since ever aroused. The splendour of his establishment, which had been the theme of ridicule among superficial observers at home, had a great effect on the minds of the British Colonists. The civilities, which no one could apply with such grace, because with such dignity, went a great way in conciliating the leaders, who were thus flattered with the belief that if they had lost some power, they had lost none of that consideration which, after all, is what vulgar minds look on as the best part of power. In a very short time Lord Durham had by these means completely gained the confidence of almost the whole British population. They looked forward with the fullest expectation of finding his measures in accordance with the feelings that he had charmed them by expressing. Our main difficulty with them arose from their wish to push their victory over their opponents further than good feeling or good policy would permit. This was the sure consequence of a dangerous and protracted conflict, and the British wished not only to disable the French so as to prevent their future aggressions, but also to wreak their revenge upon them under the forms of law.

But the state of the Lower Province was not the only subject of difficulty and anxiety. The accounts which we received from Upper Canada were from the first most alarming. The cause of the dissensions and disorders there it was not easy to understand. But it was clear that there had been very extensive and violent disaffection. It was also clear that the dominant party there had taken advantage of the recent insurrection to exercise the greatest severity towards their opponents. This had only increased the discontents, and if the tendency to actual revolt had been checked, the number of persons seriously dissatisfied with the Government was at this time far greater than it had been before the insurrection. The Governor, Sir George Arthur, a very weak and timid man, seemed to be divided between his deference for the conciliatory policy dictated by Lord Glenelg and his subservience to the violent counsels of the Family Compact, under whose influence he had completely fallen. From our first landing he sent us the most alarming accounts, one after the other, of the insurrectionary spirit of the Upper Province, and of the formidable plans as well of the refugees, who hung on its frontiers, as of the whole border population of the United States. And before the end of the month his alarms, though exaggerated, received some confirmation from the invasion and outbreak which took place under Morrow, Chandler, and others at the Short Hills in the Niagara District.

But there was quite enough in the state of our relations with the United States to inspire the boldest and calmest mind with deep apprehensions. The Canadian refugees collected along the frontier from New Hampshire to Michigan, rendered desperate by their exile and the ruin of all their prospects in life, were everywhere preparing a threatening invasion, and doing almost as much mischief to the peaceable inhabitants of the Canadas by the alarms which they thus kept up, as could have resulted from actual incursions. They kept the appearance if not the reality of an incessant correspondence with disaffected persons on our side of the frontier, and they seemed to have the support also of a general and active sympathy on the other side. It was impossible to ascertain what proportion or what class of the American public were prepared to aid the fugitives. But the lawless and wild race that peopled the frontiers, especially the shores of the Great Lakes, were evidently eager for some desperate enterprise of plunder or conquest, and these alone, in the circumstances of that time, and on that defenceless and extended line, were a formidable support to internal disaffection. At public meetings, too, the hostile language of the refugees and their less reputable associates seemed to be countenanced by persons of character and property, who might be supposed to be under the influence of political fanaticism or national antipathy. This open violence was supposed to be abetted by wealthy men who were disposed to speculate on the chances of war, and the profits of a conquest of Canada. The strong and general opinion of the respectable citizens doubtless discountenanced this aggressive spirit. But even among these there existed much sympathy with colonists supposed to be struggling against that tyranny of the Mother Country, which had driven the forefathers of the American people into revolt. Some remains of old national antipathy to Great Britain yet appeared to exist, and the insolent language in which not merely reckless individuals but even some of the authorities in Canada, especially Sir Francis Head, had denounced the people and institutions of the United States had greatly incensed many of them. A large section of the newspaper press supported the refugees and their allies, and each of the great political parties in the Union seemed occasionally disposed to recruit partisans by assuming a warlike tone towards Great Britain. It was asserted that the Government of Washington was not guiltless of encouraging these feelings, and of conniving at the most unjustifiable enterprises against the British Colonies; and it was quite clear that the Federal Executive, even if so disposed, was not very capable of putting a stop to them with sufficient decision. These evils, great in reality, were magnified tenfold by the rumours designedly spread by the many, who on each side of the frontier found their account in fomenting disturbance and alarm.

It was only three or four days after our landing that these alarms were brought to a head by the news of the burning of the *Sir Robert Peel*, a British steamer, in the American waters of the St. Lawrence by a desperate smuggler known by the name of "Bill Johnson," who had long haunted the Thousand Isles, and now appeared resolved to carry on his marauding trade under colour of Canadian "Patriotism." The alarm excited by this desperado's force or designs was, however, light in comparison with that occasioned by the chances of collision with the United States, which this outrage prevented. Immediately afterwards this alarm was increased by intelligence of another violation of the pacific relations of the two countries, which had occurred at Brockville, where British sentries had fired on a peaceable American steamboat, the *Telegraph*. The angry feeling on both sides was now raised to the highest pitch; the press indulged in the warmest recriminations, and the more violent residents on each side of the line loudly threatened their neighbours with invasion and reprisals. It seemed hardly possible to preserve peace, and I, who had up to that time indulged the most sanguine hopes of the pacification of Canada, thought that all chance of success in that object would very speedily be destroyed by the breaking out of a war between Great Britain and the United States.

Out of all this evil the vigour and sagacity of Lord Durham brought immediate and great good. On the receipt of the intelligence of the destruction of the *Sir Robert Peel,* he offered a reward of a thousand pounds to any one who should bring the offenders to trial and conviction in the courts of the United States. But while by this step he declared the determination of the British Government to protect its subjects, and thereby conciliated the goodwill of the loyal inhabitants of Canada, he took care to show the utmost respect for the Government of the United States by exhibiting his confidence in its good faith. He determined to take this opportunity of impressing on that Government the necessity of a prompt and cordial co-operation with ours for the suppression of disorders fraught with such danger to the pacific relations of the two countries. For this purpose he despatched Colonel Grey to Washington. This mission was attended with the best results. The friendly declarations of the President and Secretary of State were accompanied by substantial proofs of sincerity. The force on the borders was increased, the strict laws of neutrality recently passed by Congress were at length enforced, and within a fortnight from Colonel Grey's arrival at Washington, the forces of Great Britain and the United States were co-operating on the Lakes and St. Lawrence in repressing the disturbers of the common peace.

These precautions against the interruption of peace with the United States were our first serious business, and while harassed and occupied with this we received most discouraging news from home. Within a week from our arrival in Canada we heard of the discussions which had taken place in the House of Lords immediately after our leaving England, in reference to the appointment of Mr. Turton. The determination of the Tory peers to impair Lord Durham's authority by constant attacks in the worst spirit of faction were not nearly so discouraging as the apparent readiness of Lord Melbourne to abandon and even blame him. The despatches which we received on this subject drew forth answers from Lord Durham, in which he expressed very freely his feelings with respect to the conduct of Ministers. Thus from the outset was there distrust and ill feeling between the two parties, owing to what, if not cowardice or indifference, could only be viewed as proof of very malignant perfidy on the part of the Government. And thus, amid all the difficulties of our task on the spot, there hung over us from the first like a cloud the depressing consciousness that we had no support to rely on at home, that faction would make no allowance for the difficulties and dangers of our position, but seize hold of every pretext for discrediting and thwarting Lord Durham, and that to uphold him against such assaults he could rely on no sincerity or energy on the part of the Ministers whom he was serving.

It was, however, necessary for him to proceed in his course without faltering, and give some earnest of his intention to carry into effect the reforms which he had promised. The state of the Province and all its institutions afforded ample scope for the amending hand, and in the month of June, before our departure for Montreal and Upper Canada, Lord Durham made some considerable practical reforms. The first was the establishment of a very efficient police in Quebec, where before this there had in fact been none. This institution was immediately afterwards extended to Montreal, where the want of a good police had been quite as much felt. . . .

Among the practical grievances of the Province none was more palpable, and certainly none more injurious, than the gross mismanagement of the Crown Lands. One of Lord Durham's first objects in his Mission was to lay the foundations of such a reform in the administration of them as might render them instrumental in promoting that influx of colonists which was requisite for the accomplishment of his great schemes for the improvement of the colonies. With this end in view he had engaged Mr. Wakefield to come from England about the time of our own departure, having for some time been acquainted with him, and having completely entered into all his views of colonies and emigration. On the 18th of June he issued the Commission for an Inquiry into the state of the Crown Lands in all the North American Colonies. As Lord Glenelg, though well aware beforehand of

Mr. Wakefield's coming out with Lord Durham, had, when frightened by the discussions about Mr. Turton, written to prohibit Mr. Wakefield's being employed publicly, I was nominally placed at the head of the Commission. But my other avocations entirely prevented my taking any part in the work; the details of it were accordingly left to my Assistant Commissioner, Mr. Hanson, but the real direction of the whole business was entrusted to Mr. Wakefield, who had no ostensible employment....

The last of the practical reforms now effected, which I need mention, was rendered necessary by the limited number of an Executive Council, which imposed on Lord Durham the necessity of taking some measures with regard to the jurisdiction in Appeals from the Courts of Law of the Province. . . . He took this occasion, therefore, instead of merely completing the quorum, to constitute a really efficient Court of Appeal on sound principles. He composed it almost wholly of the highest and ablest judges of the Province. In order to keep up the necessary quorum he added Mr. Turton, whose great legal knowledge and experience rendered his presence in the Court most useful, and for the same reason he was obliged to add my brother. The Court as thus constituted held only these single sittings. But the opinion of both bar and suitors was unanimously in favour of the soundness and importance of this reform. It was agreed on all hands that so efficient a Court of Appeal had never before been seen in the Province.

But the most important and difficult task remained to be done by the disposal of the prisoners who had filled the gaols since the suppression of the insurrection. This was a matter wholly foreign to the true purpose of our Mission; it had been thrown upon us by the timidity of Sir John Colborne, who, swayed backwards and forwards, as all the authorities in the Canadas were, between the ferocity of the dominant party in the province and the more enlightened orders which came to him from England, determined to shift the responsibility of this most delicate business from himself on to Lord Durham. The difficulty of disposing of the prisoners had in no degree been diminished by the delay. It is true that the leading persons of the British party had begun

to entertain more rational and humane feelings than had animated them on the first suppression of the insurrection; and the
mass of the British, though still thirsting for some blood, were,
as the event proved, very easy to be reconciled to a lenient course.
But the difficulty of getting any punishment at all inflicted by
the verdict of a jury had been only increased by the lapse of time,
and though every one in the Province was convinced that the
allowing the prisoners to escape without any punishment would
have the most dangerous results, we felt that public opinion in
England would revolt from our having recourse to military
tribunals so long after the cessation of the insurrection and
martial law. We might, by altering the Jury law, or by using the
influence of Government over the sheriffs, have secured a British
jury, which would have convicted the innocent and guilty alike.
But besides the mischiefs of a public trial, which must have
brought to light many things that for the honour of Government
and of individuals, as well as for the best interests of order, it was
most important to bury in oblivion, and the publication of which
would probably have rendered it necessary to deal severely with
those who should be proved to have been leaders in the insurrection, we all felt that it would be far more for the permanent
interests of liberty and for the honour of the British Government
to secure the punishment of a few guilty individuals by an open
deviation for that purpose from the ordinary forms of law, than
to make new laws permanently depriving the French Canadians
of the guarantees for equal justice, or to set the dangerous prece-
dent of packing a jury.

After much deliberation on this matter, Mr. Turton and I, to
whom the investigation of the details had been left, came to the
conclusion that the best course would be to punish the leaders
certainly, but lightly, by means of an *ex post facto* law. When
this was first proposed to Lord Durham he instantly saw what
an outcry would be raised in England against an act so contrary
to our notions of liberty and law; and he refused to take any step
of the kind unless it should be requested by the prisoners themselves. The prisoners, who expected the Government to avail
itself of its power of packing a jury, and ensuring their capital

punishment, were very ready to petition to be disposed of without trial, and as I had in the meantime ascertained that the proposed mode of dealing with them would not be condemned by the leading men of the British party, Lord Durham adopted the plan proposed, and on the 28th of June, the day of Her Majesty's Coronation, issued the famous Ordinance with respect to the prisoners, and the Proclamation of Amnesty. The ultimate results of this bold step neither Lord Durham nor those with him are responsible for; its immediate effects were even more satisfactory than we had ventured to anticipate. In America its success was complete. The British population of Lower Canada, after a few partial indications of dissatisfaction, universally acquiesced in it. The French, who were not disposed to be satisfied with anything but an entire concession to all their most unreasonable views, were awed by the decision, and conciliated by the lenity of the Act. After a while they ceased to murmur at it. But its reception in the United States was most satisfactory. All parties agreed in extolling it as a noble, wise, and liberal act. The very newspapers that had previously been most violent in assailing the British Government changed their tone for a while. And the revulsion of feeling throughout the Union was general and permanent. From that hour the feelings of national jealousy and political sympathy gave way to that of admiration of Lord Durham. From that hour the disaffected in Canada ceased to derive any aid from the public opinion of our neighbours, and among our difficulties we had no longer to contend with the chance of war with the United States.

I think there was only one error with which throughout this business Lord Durham is justly chargeable, and it was an error to which I must attribute most injurious effects. He ought, in announcing such a step to the Home Government, to have given an ample and detailed statement of the grounds on which he had felt it right to compose his Special Council, and dispose of the prisoners as he had done; and I fear that to the absence of some such explanation, which might have been laid before Parliament, and served to convey a knowledge of the real state of affairs, is to be ascribed that misapprehension on these points which enabled

Lord Durham's assailants to produce any effect whatever on the public mind. The composition of our Special Council was calculated to be misunderstood by those who did not know how difficult it would have been to find any better materials in Lower Canada. If Lord Durham had fully explained the grounds of his Ordinance, the public at home would readily have appreciated his manliness in composing his Special Council so as in fact to shift no responsibility off his own shoulders. And it could easily have been shewn that had he composed the Council, as Sir John Colborne had done, of residents in the Province, he must in the existing state of things have thereby placed the power of Legislation in the hands of one party, which would assuredly have used them, as it had been done under Sir John Colborne, for the promotion of its own interests and the oppression of its opponents.

Immediately after the publication of the Ordinances, Lord Durham, accompanied by Sir Charles Paget, the Admiral on the American Station, set out for Montreal. Our departure from Quebec gave occasion for a very sullen demeanour on the part of the British inhabitants, who were by no means pleased with the lenity of the Ordinances. We heard that a still more unfavourable feeling would probably be exhibited on our arrival at Montreal. It was about the middle of the day of the 5th of July when our steamboat cast anchor opposite to that city, and we instantly received the visits of the authorities and principal inhabitants. The state of terror and uncertainty which then existed throughout the Canadas was testified to us by a hundred alarming rumours that reached us in the course of the day. The full effect of the Ordinances had not yet had time to develop itself. We had every reason to believe that the British inhabitants of Montreal, who, having been in the very midst of the preceding party struggles, had naturally contracted a greater violence of feeling than even the rest of their race in the Province, would very strongly exhibit their disapprobation of the lenity of the Ordinance. Nor had this measure had time to exhibit its effects on the public opinion of the United States, and the country was inundated with alarms of fresh demonstrations of American "sympathy" with the insurgents. I recollect well that during the twenty-four hours that elapsed between our arrival in the port and our landing, there were brought to us no less than three distinct and circumstantial accounts of "Bill Johnson's" invasion of the Provinces at the head of a large force of rebels and "sympathizers," he himself being reputed to have made his appearance at no less than three different points at the distance of about five hundred miles from each other. It had required little time to learn to give very little weight to any rumours that we might hear in Canada, and these produced little impression on us except as far as they went to convince us of the extremely disorganized state of men's minds in the province. Lord Durham had not lost the opportunity afforded him by the visits of the leaders of the British, who on their return spread the most favourable report of his views. An instant change was produced in the minds of this people, who seem to me, from all the experience I have had of them, to be, of all the English race that I have ever met with, the most excitable, and the most susceptible of new impressions. When Lord Durham landed on the 6th, the whole city poured out to meet him, and received him with the utmost enthusiasm.

We remained some days at Montreal, and it was here that Lord Durham, in a private interview with a large number of the British leaders, developed for the first time an outline of his views with respect to the permanent settlement of the Colonies. . . . In the answers to the various addresses which he received from different bodies, Lord Durham availed himself of the opportunity of making known the general principles on which he meant to administer the government of the Province. He well knew to what account he could turn these occasions of ceremony, and his answers were all framed with the same great principles in view, the various aspects of which the various addresses enabled him to bring before the public. The chord which he touched in addressing all these bodies was the determination of Great Britain to uphold her connexion with these Provinces, of which he painted the vast resources, and the ease with which they might be developed. By the consideration of their common interest in this he urged both parties to union and tranquillity, and, while he impressed on the one the necessity of co-operating in the reform of their defective laws, and of casting aside the petty jealousies of race, he exhorted the other to an oblivion of the insurrection, and of the long course of irritating events that had preceded it.

On the 10th we left Montreal, and soon entered Upper Canada, where during our progress up the river Lord Durham received addresses from the various towns which we passed, indicative, in spite of the violent dissensions that existed in the Province, of a pretty unanimous resolution to confide in him. But every step that we took in this province showed us the fearful extent and nature of the divisions that separated classes and parties. . . .

We passed unharmed and unassailed through the romantic region of the Thousand Isles, where indeed nature seemed to have invited the attempts of "Bill Johnson" and his gang; and went straight to the Falls of Niagara, where Lord Durham had very wisely ordered a considerable display of military force to be made. At this spot, the general rendezvous at this season of large numbers of travellers of the wealthy class of the United States, the reviews which now took place attracted a crowd of spectators from the opposite side; and the presence of the Governor-General, of the authorities of Upper Canada, of the Admiral, and of a numerous and most efficient military force of every kind was calculated to impress on our neighbours the value which the British Government was disposed to attach to the maintenance of her empire in the Canadas, and of the efficient means by which that determination was backed. The hospitalities that Lord Durham very widely extended to the visitors from the United States, were productive of even more useful results, because they excited in them better feelings than the mere dread of our arms. After the studied reserve that it had been usual for the leading persons in the British provinces to maintain towards their republican neighbours, it was most gratifying to the latter to be received with cordiality by the nobleman of the highest position with whom they had ever come in contact. I have often said to those who (after the fashion of petty carping, by which we were assailed) used to dilate on the seven or eight hundred pounds that were spent in the course of Lord Durham's visit to Niagara as a monstrous expense, that, considering the results attributable to it, a million of money would have been a cheap price for the single glass of wine which Lord Durham drank to the health of the American President. For such had been the absurd demeanour of the authorities in the British Colonies towards those of the United States that it actually seemed as if the latter Government were not completely recognized by ours. This mere ordinary civility, therefore, on the part of the Governor-General was taken by the Americans present, and by their countrymen at large, as indicative of a thorough change of feeling and policy, and as a pledge of goodwill towards their country. Of the change thereby produced in their feelings, we had speedy and gratifying proofs, and these acts of civility created among the mass that regard for Lord Durham which the wise and humane policy of his government had in great measure already produced among the more thinking. Henceforth, instead of incivilities being offered to every British officer who chanced to cross the lines, the citizens of the United States vied with each other in hospitality and respect to them. Lord Durham continued this wise course after his return to Quebec, where he made a point of receiving the numerous travellers from the United States at his house during the summer. These were in themselves but slight acts and easy observances, but they were parts of a great view of international relations, and produced great and good effects on the feelings and intercourse of two nations. It is only the man of statesmanlike mind who can produce a great result out of things so small as an invitation to dinner, or the drinking a glass of wine. . . .

In the short period which had elapsed between our first arrival in Lower Canada and our return from the Upper Province, a very great and beneficial change had already been wrought in the state of things. The change in our position with respect to the United States was the most important; no imminent risk of war any longer harassed us and deranged our plans; on the contrary, the favourable feeling of the States came to the aid of our Government and operated for us in public opinion in Canada. The British party, in spite of the secret dissatisfaction of some of its leaders, had very generally rallied round Lord Durham. The French had become somewhat more reconciled to their lot, and though secret intrigues still continued to be carried on among *habitans*, the change of feeling in the United States had convinced the leaders of the refugees, as well as of the disaffected in the province, that their main support, which had been the sympathy of their neighbours, was altogether withdrawn. . . .

The multitudinous business of the more ordinary administration of the Province of Lower Canada occupied of course much of Lord Durham's time. Every question of magnitude that arose in British North America was referred to him. The disposal of the political prisoners in Upper Canada was the subject of a long and warm correspondence with Sir George Arthur. An application to Lord Durham from the wives of Chandler and Waite, two of the unhappy men condemned to death for what was called the Short Hills insurrection, occasioned his interference in the first instance. This was somewhat angrily resented by Sir George Arthur. I need not enter into the particulars of a discussion which is contained in the correspondence printed at the end of Ridgway's edition of the Report, and which does honour to Lord Durham's humanity as well as to his political wisdom. The result was most satisfactory, for after earnest entreaties from Sir George Arthur to be allowed to execute at first four, and then at least one of the convicts, the lives of all these unhappy men were saved, and what was even more important, Sir George Arthur was induced to proclaim a General Amnesty, by which the fears of the various families compromised in the late risings were set at rest, and the greater part of the political exiles, who molested the frontier, were permitted to return, and became harmless at home. . . .

Lord Durham, before leaving England, had, with a view principally to having some definite subject of discussion with the persons whom he might consult in the Province, prepared the outline of a plan for the future government, founded on suggestions which he had received both from public documents and discussions, and from individuals who had paid a great attention to the subject. Soon after his arrival in Canada he had taken advantage of visits from the Lieutenant-Governors of what are commonly called the Lower Provinces, to desire them to send to Quebec such persons of every party in their respective Colonies as they might consider capable of giving the soundest opinion on such a subject. Accordingly, on the 12th of September, deputations from Nova Scotia and Prince Edward's Island came to Quebec, and in a few days after arrived that from New Brunswick. Great praise is due to the Governors for the skill and impartiality with which they selected the deputations. Their members appeared to have been very fairly selected as the ablest representatives of the different parties in the Colonies. They gave us indeed a very favourable opinion of the state of society in the Lower Provinces. Generally men of plain manners, they exhibited also a great deal of plain good sense and fairness. Opposed in provincial politics they could discuss even their own points of difference with candour and moderation. The deputation from Nova Scotia in particular pleased us highly. Some of its leading members were persons not only of striking ability, but of a degree of general information and polish of manners which are even less commonly met with in colonial society. . . .

Our conferences with the deputations were harmonious and satisfactory. I need not now specify the effects produced on our opinions by these discussions, nor how it was that our views (for it was so not only with Lord Durham, but with all of us) gradually took the shape in which they were embodied in the Report. The urgency of an union was more forcibly impressed on our minds in the course of our conferences, and still more by subsequent events. And as we discussed the details of a plan, so the merits of a federal scheme faded away by degrees, and we became convinced of the propriety of such a complete legislative union of the provinces as was afterwards proposed in Lord Durham's Report. The language held by the deputation showed us that the public mind of all the Provinces was prepared for an Union, and that such a measure would be conducive to their separate interests as well as to the common good of the empire.

In the midst of these occupations we received the astounding news of the disallowance of the Ordinance of the 28th of June. Previous intelligence had by no means prepared us for this. Lord Durham had received not only a dispatch from Lord Glenelg, but also an autograph letter from the Queen highly approving of the Ordinance. We had no reason to believe from the reports of the first debates on the subject in Parliament that any person would join Lord Brougham and Mr. Leader in their outcry against the Ordinance. Lord Durham had always had misgivings as to the result. I will own that I had felt none. I thought that the merciful and pacifying purpose of the Act would have so pleased the great mass of our countrymen that there would have been no dissent from their universal approbation. I still think that I judged the mass of my countrymen aright, and that by them Lord Durham's Ordinances were fairly appreciated and fully approved. But he counted more accurately than I did on the selfishness of parties and the consequences of intrigue. I recollect well the day that the news arrived. I happened, amid my usual fatigues, to have that morning a few hours of leisure, and at Lord Durham's request I went with him on an excursion in the neighbourhood. The incidents of this little journey are fresh in my recollection even now; I well remember what we saw, and how we talked, and how we laughed under the bright Canadian sky in that fine autumn day. As I was walking back from the carriage to my lodgings some one told me the news in general terms, but I supposed it to originate either in joke or in mistake, and hardly thought again about it. However, when I got into the carriole to go with Mr. Turton to dinner, he told me that the report was quite true, and when I arrived at the house Lord Durham sent for me, told me the news, and, almost more by manner than words, let me know that his mind was made up to resign his government. I saw indeed from the first that such would inevitably be the result, and that here—for a while at least—was destroyed the whole fabric of improvement that Lord Durham had with so much labour and anxiety been building up during the period of his government.

Whenever up to this time the least mention had been made of

resignation, I had invariably combated it as a thing not to be for a moment thought of. I had recently done this with great warmth; I had represented the trust confided to Lord Durham as similar to that of the defence of some besieged outpost of the empire, and I had asserted that in his case, as in that of the military commandant, success would be the only proof that our countrymen would accept of the efficiency of his defence. Great, unexpectedly great, as was the additional discouragement to which he was now exposed, I think—I even then thought—that it would have been wise, had it been possible, for Lord Durham to have held his post. His reasons for quitting it have been stated at full length in his dispatches and proclamation, and they unanswerably show the fearful chances of failure in his great purpose of maintaining and pacifying Canada, to which the factious conduct of the Tories and the more fatal abandonment of Ministers had exposed him. I think also that they quite clearly showed that the persecution of which Lord Durham had been the object from the outset of his government, and the mistrust of his power occasioned by the recent occurrences, had placed difficulties in his way from which another governor would in all likelihood be free. Still I think that had he met the difficulties with his accustomed energy, he would in all probability have succeeded, and that the honour and advantage of success after such discouragement would have been so great that it would have been quite prudent for such a prize to run the risk of a failure for which under the circumstances of the case nobody could have blamed him. I approved of his resignation on a ground which now, alas! I may very plainly mention. Without surmising the real nature or extent of the mischief, I saw that Lord Durham's health was fearfully affected by all that had passed. Such a degree of nervous agitation did his disease produce, and such a reaction of that agitation on his bodily health was constantly going on, that it was evidently impossible for him to bear up against the anxieties and labour of his government under existing circumstances, and display that energy and promptitude of decision which had so eminently distinguished him when his health was better. I felt convinced—and unhappily it is now too clear that I was likely to be right—that Lord Durham's life would very soon have been the sacrifice for his continuance in Canada, even for two or three months, and that at any rate he was liable to have his energies impaired by illness at moments in which any relaxation of them would have been fatal to success. I lamented his resignation then: I deplore it yet more deeply now; but I approved of it then, and approve of it now as an act done in compliance with a stern and sad necessity. I must not be understood as admitting that his return home was calculated to injure the interests of the Province; on the contrary, I still think that in the difficulties then impending the preservation of the Province was more *safe* in the hands of Sir John Colborne than in those of Lord Durham, weakened as they were by the repeated proofs of his being unsupported at home. It is for his own sake—for the sake of the influence which his continuance in his government under such circumstances would have ensured him—and for the sake of all the strength that would thence have accrued to the popular cause at home, that I regret that the state of his health compelled him to abandon this chance of fame and power, and that even this sacrifice came too late to avert the blow which disease had already struck.

The declaration of Lord Durham's intended resignation spread terror and grief throughout British North America. The delegates from the Lower Provinces gave utterance to the first expression of regret at his departure, and of entreaty that he would remain, and it was in answer to them that he first publicly announced his intention of resigning. In consequence of this, addresses of a similar nature came from all parts of both the Canadas. The address from Quebec, presented in the hall of the House of Assembly, gave occasion to a burst of the most enthusiastic popular feeling. Large deputations brought the addresses from Kingston, Toronto, and Montreal, and expressed the alarm with which the whole British race in Canada regarded the attacks made on Lord Durham, and the consequent calamity of his resignation. The French—though some of the more honest and sagacious of their leaders were inclined to express openly their regret at an event, which deprived them of their own efficient protection from the violence of their antagonists—maintained their usual sullen and impassive demeanour. But the feeling and the movement of deep regret extended throughout the British of every party in the two provinces. Even those who had the most violently condemned his policy—even the most reckless of the Family Compact of Upper Canada—expressed the common feeling in terms proving how sincerely they participated in alarm at Lord Durham's departure, if not in approval of his policy.

These demonstrations did not, however, affect the grounds on which Lord Durham and all around him saw that his resignation was absolutely necessary. Indeed these considerations, together with the news which reached us from every quarter of the preparations for fresh insurrection, rendered it incumbent on Lord Durham at once to put the fact of his resolution beyond a doubt, and to take measures for his instant departure, in order to end that species of interregnum which cannot but exist when a governor has declared his intention of giving up his office. With this view, he determined on leaving the Province at the close of October, and he announced this by the famous Proclamation which he issued on the 9th of that month.

In this Proclamation Lord Durham had two great objects in view. The first was that of calming the excessive agitation which his abrupt departure from Canada had occasioned, by showing that he did not despair, and that he yet hoped by immediate and energetic remonstrances at home to effect that good which he could not secure by remaining in Canada. The second was certainly that of vindicating himself by the only public means in his power. He has been much censured for publishing what has been considered an inflammatory appeal from the Imperial Government and Legislature to the people of the Colonies. It must not, however, be matter of surprise that after the unusual mode in which Lord Durham had been assailed in Parliament and abandoned by the Ministry—after his policy had been condemned without hearing or explanation, that he should think it necessary to step somewhat beyond the line of official usage, in order to protect himself against those who had used him thus ungenerously. As for the inflammatory effect which it has been said that the proclamation was calculated, if not intended, to produce, the answer simply is that it both purported to seek, and did in effect produce, precisely the opposite result. No disorder, no increase of disaffection ensued; on the contrary, all parties in the Province expressed a revival of confidence; and we had it very clearly shown to us that one effect of the Proclamation had been that of inducing a much more general readiness to enlist in the volunteer corps, and take other measures for the defence of the provinces.

There was, however, one necessary consequence of the great hurry in which Lord Durham was compelled to take his departure when once determined on, that I much regretted. He had originally purposed embarking at New York, after previously visiting Washington. The knowledge of this intention had created the greatest satisfaction in the United States, and the people had made preparations for giving him an enthusiastic welcome. Shortly after, in my passage through the States, I heard that the corporations of the various great cities on his line of way had made arrangements for meeting him at different points, and conveying him from one to the other. In fact he was everywhere to be received by the local authorities as a public visitor. On our return to England he was informed by Mr. Stevenson, the American Minister, that at Washington he was to have remained with the President at the White House as a national guest—an honour never before conferred on any one but Lafayette. Such a deep impression had Lord Durham made on the people of the United States: nor has that impression been yet effaced: to the hour of his death his popularity in that great country remained undiminished. I regret that no visible exhibition of this popularity occurred in the manner proposed, both because it would have been a great support to Lord Durham at home, and because it would have been useful in teaching our public men in what way and with what ease mere honesty and courtesy can secure the goodwill of that great kindred nation. But the intimations of meditated insurrection were so numerous and strong that Lord Durham felt that he must lose no time in returning home, and that it would be unseemly in him to be travelling in the United States at a time in which the seat of his late government might probably be a prey to civil war.

During the short time that remained before his departure, he occupied himself in bringing to a close or advancing the various inquiries and reform which he had commenced. . . .

It was on the 1st of November that Lord Durham sailed from Quebec in the *Inconstant*. A sad day and sad departure it was. The streets were crowded; the spectators filled every window and every house-top; and, though every hat was raised as we passed, a deep silence marked the general grief for Lord Durham's departure. His own presentiments depressed him, and those about him, for he had told me and others also that he did not expect to reach England alive. When I left him (for I had to stay some time behind to collect materials for the Report) I had as a member of the Executive Council to repair to the Castle, where Sir John Colborne was to be sworn in. There were but few people in the room, but the countenances of the old Executive Councillors seemed to mark the restoration of the ancient system of administration. A good many military officers also were present; they seemed to think that their ascendancy also was restored. The ceremony was silently hurried over, and when it was finished I went to the window, which commanded a full view of the harbour. The cannon were just sounding in honour of his successor's installation, when the frigate that bore Lord Durham was slowly towed out of the harbour. The sky was black with clouds bearing the first snowstorm of the winter, and hardly a breath of air was moving. I returned to my office, and, some hours after, from the window, which commanded the wide basin below the city, I saw the dark form of that ill-omened ship slowly, and as it were painfully, struggling on its course. My heart filled with many a bitter regret, many a superstitious presentiment, and alas! many too true misgiving. We dined that evening at Mr. Daly's, and the party was composed of Mr. Turton, my brother, and myself, forming with him the last remains of Lord Durham's government. It was a mournful meeting, and none mourned more deeply than our kind and honourable host, who said that with Lord Durham's departure all his hope had gone. A heavy fall of snow was setting in as we left the house, and the very morning after the winter was completely set in. The next day we heard the alarming report that Lord Durham's worst forebodings had been nigh being fulfilled in the most fearful manner by a fire on board the ship. This was perfectly true; not so the reports which reached us every now and then during the next fortnight to the effect that Lord Durham had been forced to put into Halifax, or that he had been driven ashore on some other part of the coast. After fearful perils at the outset, the *Inconstant* kept on her course to its appointed end amid almost perpetual storms, which did not cease even when she had reached the shelter of Plymouth Sound.

Thus ended Lord Durham's Mission to Canada, and instead of bringing these great results to the country, and that harvest of honour and power to himself, which we had hoped, and for which we had all laboured, it seemed at its close to have ended in nothing but disappointment to all concerned in it. Its most fatal consequence, indeed, was his feeling that disappointment so acutely, and that, sickened by the malignity and weakness of which he had been the victim, he from the hour of his return gave way to a depression that quickened the progress of his malady. Many of those who enthusiastically rallied around him on his return, have since reproached him that he threw away the opportunity of complete justification and satisfaction, and refused to take that position in the political world which seemed to invite him. But this course he took after full and anxious consideration, and took I think as wisely as I am sure he did it honestly. Abstaining from all public part in general politics, he reserved himself for Canada alone. Nor did he seek to urge on the discussion of that topic. When Lord Winchelsea imprudently attempted to renew his persecution of Mr. Turton, Lord Durham's short and vigorous speech scared his assailants, and at once and forever checked all similar attacks. From that hour he remained unmolested by those who had been so eager in assailing him during his absence. He never in his turn became the assailant. Public opinion had done him such complete justice in the matter of the

Ordinance that, if he had brought it again before Parliament, it must have been for the purpose of assault, not of self-defence. When at the close of the session the question of the future government of Canada came before the House of Lords, he contented himself with a short speech, in which he neither defended himself nor attacked others, but, approving of the policy of ministers in postponing final legislation on the subject, emphatically impressed on the House of Lords the principles on which he thought that their conduct towards Canada ought to be shaped. At the moment, perhaps, the vindication of measures unjustly condemned and thwarted, and the triumphant assertion of his own policy by dint of argument and eloquence, might have given more satisfaction to his friends. But now we may with far higher and purer pride look back to the forbearance which he displayed, recollecting that, when all others thought most of his personal position and wrongs, he said nothing of them. True to the public principles of his past life, he allowed no impulse of anger, no scheme of ambitious aggrandizement out of the many assiduously suggested to him, to turn him from the course which, independently of all personal considerations, he judged to be the best calculated to serve his country. To the last day of his life his influence was steadily and effectually employed in repressing those feelings on the part of his political friends which, if uncontrolled by him, would on many an occasion have given the finishing blow to the existence of Lord Melbourne's ministry. More active exertions in the general field of politics, and the consequent attainment of the power of more effectually serving his country in office, we might have expected, had he possessed the health which had been the spring of his former energy. This it pleased Providence to deny us; but his hard fate could not deprive him, during the period that followed his return from Canada, of the opportunity of exhibiting a generous forbearance and an unselfish love of country.

Nor need we look with any dissatisfaction at the fruits of his Mission. That these were at first less obvious and less abundant than they should have been was not his fault, but that of those whose misconduct cut short the brilliant and useful career of his

144

administration, and compelled him to leave to others the execution and completion of what he had only planned or commenced. The period of his government, which seems so long when we follow its various incidents and acts, was after all but of five months' duration, and yet in that short time what great practical results did he bring about! His policy in fact it was that pacified Canada and secured its retention. He found the gaols of Lower Canada full of prisoners trembling for their lives, which had been forfeited to the law, and the frontiers crowded with hopeless and reckless exiles. These traces of insurrection he removed, freed every prisoner, and recalled the exiles, without shedding any man's blood or confiscating any man's estate. In Upper Canada, where he could not so speedily or completely exercise his authority to the same effect, he nevertheless succeeded in producing nearly similar results by his advice and example. He found the British of Lower Canada suspicious and angry: he inspired them with confidence. He found the great mass of the people of Upper Canada animated by a discontent which bordered on disaffection, and utterly despairing of justice from Great Britain. He rallied them around the British Crown with that unanimous feeling which they since exhibited during the winter of 1838-9, when the whole population turned out against the invaders, and not a man, or hardly a man, of those most inclined to disaffection in the former troubles lent the slightest aid to the attack. He found a still more serious cause of alarm in the alienation of the great body, and the active hostility of a dangerous portion, of the people of the United States. He entirely changed the public opinion of the United States with respect to Canada; he turned it from assailing to supporting the British Government; and he so completely destroyed all general or open disposition to aid the insurgent Canadians, that, although some outrages were committed by the few reckless desperadoes who crossed the frontier at Prescott and Sandwich, the refugees and their adherents never again with any effect made an appeal to the sympathy of the American people. And though it was impossible for him to conciliate the long estranged goodwill of the French Canadians, or to eradicate their insane aspirations after the ascendancy of their race, he deprived their discontent of every justification, and so stripped them of all aid that their second insurrection exhibited only their utter want both of resources in themselves and allies without. . . .

But unquestionably the most important purpose of the mission was that of effecting, or rather suggesting, such improvements in the constitution and general administration of government in Canada, as might guard us against the recurrence of the disorders that had for many years afflicted both Provinces. This task remained to be performed when Lord Durham returned to England, and it has been completely performed in his Report. The praise of laborious inquiry and of comprehensive thought has never yet been refused to this document by those even who have most loudly condemned it. For it has been bitterly condemned by Tories, whose narrow and slavish notions its free principles of government could not but shock. It has been condemned by those whose attachment to the routine of our Colonial policy has been revolted by the startling recommendation of a generous confidence in the good sense of the people of the Colonies. It has given great offence to those Ministers whose whole recent system of Colonial policy it showed to have been shallow and unsound. And there are some, who can dispute no position in it, who cannot deny the truth of its statements of the general soundness of its conclusions, but who, being of that school of wily statesmen that imagine political wisdom to consist in going round about to one's end—that regard truths as mischiefs to be suppressed, or at any rate as dangerous matters to be kept only for Cabinets and Saloons—regret that Lord Durham should have said anything about Responsible Government, or at any rate that what he said should have been published to the world. We may console ourselves that the public at large while admitting the truth of Lord Durham's views, have not shrunk from them as dangerous on that account. Even amid the universal indifference with which the Colonies are regarded here, the public in this country have generally and highly approved of the Report. But in the Colonies it has become the textbook of every advocate of colonial freedom, of every one who denies that our countrymen in the Colonies should have that voice in their own government which Englishmen are used to regard as the birthright of their race. In Canada it has become the rallying-point of the great body of the people; those whom the ancient misgovernment had driven to the verge of disaffection have waived all their former objects for that of the practical adoption of Lord Durham's Report, and under his name every subdivision of the friends of liberal government have united as "Durhamites," and insist on that which he sanctioned and no more. Nor has the Report been less studied or adopted in the other Colonies. The people of the West Indies and of the Cape of Good Hope have claimed the benefit of its principles, and every newspaper from the various Colonies of the Australasian World appeals to it as the manual of Colonial Reform.

Nor need we repine at the practical effect already given to the suggestions of the Report. Many of these indeed put forward rather what were views of ultimate and possible improvement, and general principles of Colonial Administration, than what can be regarded as positive recommendations for direct and immediate legislation. But the Report did distinctly and earnestly urge the Legislative Union of the two Canadas, and the principal purpose of the Act of the last Session goes to give effect to this recommendation. I think I see in the Lower Provinces a tendency towards such an accession to the present Union as would realize Lord Durham's splendid scheme of a great British community in North America. The principle of executive responsibility which he recommended, not with the vain notion that it could be enforced by positive law, but as the sure and only foundation of a firm and peaceable government of the Colonies, though repudiated in words, has been already partially recognized in the appointments made by the Government. But it does not matter very much what the Government repudiates or what it recognizes, for certain it is that in the Parliament of Upper Canada it has created a power from which no Government in this country will be able to withhold that voice in the selection of its rulers, which Lord Durham showed to be a necessary consequence of representative institutions.

If then the Mission to Canada must ever be an object of mournful contemplation to us who loved Lord Durham and lament his irreparable loss, yet, when we look to the interests of his reputation, we may regard the execution of this high and difficult task as among the noblest of the many noble memorials of his career. Let us remember that, if he failed to obtain the results of immediate satisfaction and credit to himself, it was because he laboured for higher and more permanent objects. In this, as in every other part of his course through life, he left the trodden path of old routine and bygone systems, and was the first to advance towards whatever of wider and clearer views the enlarged experience of mankind has in these days reached. Here, as in other matters, his foresight enabled him to base his policy on those principles on which the coming age of the world will be ruled. He who acts thus must not expect that he will be rightly appreciated by the little knots of intrigues, from whose thoughts and interests he separates himself. But from the mass of his countrymen he may expect at least that generous sympathy with the rectitude of his purpose, which Lord Durham found even in his own day. From after times he will receive a yet larger meed of justice. For, as coming events in their appointed course shall prove the sagacity with which he foresaw them—as the public mind, gradually opening to new and sound views, shall be prepared to read the right lesson in the occurrences which it may witness—so will shine forth with daily increasing brightness the character of that statesman, who alone in his day rightly appreciated the worth of our Colonial Empire, and saw on what deep and sure foundations of freedom its prosperity might be reared. With us, then, that sorrow for his loss, which no time can efface, need be mingled with no vain and injurious regrets for the result of his labours, which will long survive in the bettered lot and grateful recollections of our Colonies, with none for a fame which, instead of being laid in his untimely grave, will date from the hour of his death the commencement of a long and vigorous existence.

There is one passage in the Proclamation, of which the propriety has been much questioned even by some of those most inclined to judge favourably of Lord Durham's conduct. It is that passage in which he states that, the Ordinances having been disallowed, there existed no impediment to the return of the persons who had been sent to Bermuda, or prevented from returning to the province. This was regarded by many as a mere outbreak of temper on Lord Durham's part, and it was supposed that, in order to throw obloquy on the Government at home, he actually invited dangerous persons to return to the colony. I confess that at first sight the passage in question has this appearance, and therefore I feel bound in justice to say that on that very ground Lord Durham was very reluctant to insert this passage, which I suggested, and very earnestly and perseveringly pressed on him. But practical considerations, totally unconnected with any reference to the conduct of the Home Government, induced me to make the suggestion, and, I think, justified Lord Durham in adopting it.

The instant that the news of the disallowance reached Canada, it was supposed that some of the exiles would enter the province. It seemed doubtful whether in that case they would be liable to be tried for their original offence. Nobody could deny that they had undergone *some* punishment, however inadequate, and the sound principle of *Non bis in idem* seemed, therefore, applicable to their case. But this point just admitted of so much doubt, as to make it quite certain that criminals so obnoxious to a large and violent party would not be allowed to re-establish themselves quietly at their former abodes, without some proceedings against them being attempted. We felt quite sure that they would be arrested, and that half the Magistrates in the Province would be eager to commit them for trial. The Grand Juries would have found Bills, the trials must have taken place, and then would have recurred all the mischiefs which the Ordinances had been designed to avert. The angry passion of the past insurrection would have been revived by the proceedings in the courts, the guilt of the prisoners would have been proved in the clearest manner, and there would have infallibly followed a verdict of acquittal in the face of evidence.

The punishment of the exiles could only have been secured by suspending the Habeas Corpus, or by altering the constitution of the Tribunals by either substituting Courts Martial for the ordinary Courts of Criminal Law, or packing the juries. The last Lord Durham did not choose to do, and the two former courses (though defensible in certain emergencies) appeared most unadvisable in the circumstances of the case. He had abstained from having recourse to such encroachments on constitutional principles and personal rights, when the difficulty of disposing of the prisoners had first presented itself to him in all its magnitude on his arrival in the Province; and he was most averse, for the sake of punishing a *few*, to take a course from which he had shrunk when it would have enabled him to punish *all* the guilty. And it should always be borne in mind that the measures of rigour, which may be most necessary *during* an insurrection, may be the most unadvisable when insurrection is apprehended. At that time to have suspended the Habeas Corpus, or substituted Courts Martial for Juries, would simply have been to supply the disaffected with a pretext for rebellion which we knew them to be meditating; and, what was more, give them some chance of success by setting public opinion in the United States against the Government of Canada. These were evils not even to be risked except for the most important objects, and the exiles in question were mostly so insignificant, that the keeping them out of the Province really was a matter of no consequence. As for Papineau, the only one among them of any consideration, we had learnt enough of his character to feel assured that his presence among the disaffected would have been the surest means of paralysing their operations. Besides which, however great his moral culpability, I knew that the evidence in the possession of Government, all of which I had gone through, would not in his case have justified a legal conviction.

The evils, which appeared thus likely to result from the return of the exiles, rendered it imperative on us to take some precautions to avert them. We were perfectly sure that some of the exiles would return without permission the moment that they heard of the disallowance of the Ordinances, and the fact is that one or two actually did return before the Proclamation was out. After the first step taken against any of them after their return, the consequences could have been beyond Lord Durham's control, and as he could not bring himself to commit the Government to an arbitrary course for the purpose of punishing a score of persons, he would have no choice but of letting matters run their course of arrest, trial, and unjust acquittal.

The great thing then was to prevent any step being taken against the exiles, and as they were sure to obtain impunity in the end, to let them have it at once without all the inervening excitement, and without bringing the administration of justice into further contempt. I therefore pressed on Lord Durham to take the bull by the horns, and as he knew that he could not punish the exiles if they came back, at once to tell them that there was nothing to prevent their doing so. By taking this course Lord Durham did in fact avoid all the excitement, exposure, recrimination, and subversion of justice which would have followed from his doing nothing; and, on the other hand, the worse mischief which would have resulted from his having recourse to violent exceptional measures. When the subsequent insurrection did break out, the rebels could allege no harsh act on the part of the Government as a provocation. And what was the practical mischief that resulted from letting these people back? None, that I ever heard of. None of those that returned did any harm, or even, as I firmly believe, took any part in the subsequent insurrection. But those who remained out of the province did all the harm they could.

Of course it is always an evil in the way of example, if notoriously guilty persons enjoy perfect impunity. I trust, however, that I have shown that punishing the persons in question by any unconstitutional means would have produced far worse effects even than their going unpunished.

In order to keep up the confidence of the loyal portion of the Canadian public in himself personally and generally in the Provincial Government, it was necessary for Lord Durham to point out that the impunity of these guilty and obnoxious persons was not his doing, but that of the Home Government. He could say this with perfect justice, for he had done his best to punish; his measures had been defeated by the interference of Parliament, and the present difficulty had been created solely by the disallowance of the Ordinances. And I think that it was quite as much in accordance with sound policy as with justice for him to lay the blame on Parliament. For as blame must in the opinion of the Colonists rest on some portion of the Government, it was far better that it should rest on the House than the Provincial Government. A little more discredit thrown on the proceedings of Parliament could hardly produce any sensible effect in augmenting the odium which at that moment rested on that body in the opinion of the Colonists. But anything that cast suspicion on the policy of the Provincial Government would have seriously increased the practical difficulties which surrounded not only Lord Durham, but also his successor. In Parliament the Colonists had no confidence, in the Provincial authorities an entire trust, and it would have been very unwise to weaken the influence of the latter by subjecting them to any part of the blame which Parliament and the Home Government alone deserved.

At any rate, as I began by saying, the course pursued by Lord Durham in this matter and the passage in the Proclamation were both adopted at my urgent suggestion; and I, not he, am answerable for what was done, as well as for the way in which it was announced. He was, of course, obliged to depend greatly on me with respect to all that concerned the internal administration of the Province, and more particularly in matters connected with the administration of justice. If my advice was wrong, he could not be blamed for acting by it in such matters.

I am bound to take on myself whatever blame is due to me, for well I know he never would have it cast on me. Every man who has to act on a great variety of matters of importance must rely on those whom he employs and trusts; and Lord Durham was necessarily compelled in much that he did to rely on me and act on my advice. Some steps that he took at my suggestion were among those that were most fiercely assailed either at home or in Canada. Yet never have I any reason to believe that he threw on me even the blame that I deserved. Never certainly, though often he might justly have done so, did he reproach me with the consequences of my counsels, never at least but once, in a moment of very natural excitement, and then he repaired the reproach in half an hour.

Wherever possible, quotations have been taken from the original documents in the Durham, Lambton and Grey collections, occasionally from photocopies in the Public Archives of Canada. Contemporary reports in newspapers and elsewhere, now in the Public Archives of Canada, have also been used. The most useful modern biography was published in 1929 by Chester New. *Crisis in the Canadas* 1838-39, edited by William Ormsby and published in 1964, contains a valuable collection of Col. Charles Grey's letters to his father, Earl Grey, together with an account of his experiences in Canada during the period of Lord Durham's mission. In his recent biography of Melbourne, published in 1976, Philip Ziegler has a good deal that is new to say about Lord Melbourne, and this in turn helps to explain his attitude to Durham and the Canadian crisis. The following abbreviations have been used: Durham Papers, Public Archives of Canada (D.P.); Grey Papers, Public Archives of Canada (G.P.); Lambton Collection, Chester-le-Street, County Durham (L.MSS.); Grey of Howick Collection, University of Durham (G. of H.MSS); *Aberdeen-Lieven Correspondence* (*A/L Corr.*); *Greville Journal* (*G.J.*).

[1]John George Lambton, 1st Earl of Durham (1792-1840). Eldest son of William Henry Lambton, MP for the city of Durham and Lady Anne Barbara Frances Villiers, second daughter of George, 4th Earl of Jersey. In 1797 inherited the estate which had been in the family since the 12th century. Educated at Eton. Served briefly in the army, but entered the House of Commons as a Whig MP for Co. Durham in 1813. In 1821 proposed a motion for parliamentary reform based on the formation of electoral districts, household suffrage and triennial parliaments. His motion was defeated. Created a Baron in 1828 and

entered the House of Lords. Became a member of the Privy Council and appointed Lord Privy Seal in the government of Charles, 2nd Earl Grey (note 4), father of Durham's second wife, Lady Louisa Grey. Together with Lord John Russell (note 61), Lord Duncannon and Sir James Graham, he began preparation on the first Reform Bill, the draft of which was adopted by the Cabinet in 1831 (with the exception of Durham's proposal of vote by ballot). Durham favoured passage of the Reform Bill through the House of Lords by creating a sufficient number of favourable peers. This method did not meet with Lord Grey's approval and led to some serious altercation between them. Durham was appointed Ambassador Extraordinary to St. Petersburg in July 1832, and to Berlin and Vienna in September. He returned to England the following month. Ill health forced his resignation from the Cabinet in 1833 and he was created Viscount Lambton and Earl of Durham. Grey was anxious for his return to a Cabinet post but was opposed by Lord Brougham (note 93) and Lord Lansdowne. A bitter quarrel ensued with the former after Lord Brougham attacked the Radical section of the Whig party, of which he himself, with Durham, had been an ardent supporter. In 1835 Durham was again appointed Ambassador Extraordinary and Minister Plenipotentiary to St. Petersburg where he remained until his resignation in 1837. In March 1838 he was appointed Governor General of British North America. See further notes to follow from this date until his resignation and return to England in November 1838.

In 1812 Lambton eloped to Gretna Green and married Miss Harriet Cholmondeley, the natural daughter of George, 4th Earl of Cholmondeley. Harriet died of tuberculosis in 1815. By this marriage he had three daughters, all of whom died of the same disease: Georgina Sarah Elizabeth and Harriet Caroline who died in their teens in 1832, and Frances Charlotte, who married the Hon. George Ponsonby (afterwards 5th Earl of Bessborough) and died in 1835 at the age of 23. In 1816 he married Lady Louisa Elizabeth Grey eldest daughter of Charles, 2nd Earl Grey, by whom he had two sons: Charles William, born in 1818, who also died of tuberculosis aged 13, and George

Frederick D'Arcy (note 31) and three daughters, Mary Louisa (note 7), Emily Augusta (note 88) and Alice Anne Caroline (note 15).

2. ²The uprising of November 1837 against the British government, represented by Lord Gosford (note 47) as Governor and High Commissioner, by *Les Patriotes*, a French Canadian organization under the ultimate leadership of Louis-Joseph Papineau in Lower Canada, and by the Reformers, chiefly influenced by William Lyon Mackenzie, in Upper Canada. The rebellion was the result of ethnic conflicts, lack of satisfactory Canadian representation with adequate powers, and also of frustration brought about by the severe commercial and agricultural depression of 1833-38. The actual violence was quickly repressed, but the causes, which were of long standing, continued to smoulder.

3. ³Lady Mary Elizabeth, Countess Grey (d. 1861). Mother of Lady Durham, wife of Charles, 2nd Earl Grey, and daughter of Lord William Brabazon, 1st Baron Ponsonby of Imokilly. By her marriage there were 10 sons, of whom 8 survived to adulthood, and 5 daughters.

4. ⁴Charles, 2nd Earl Grey (1764-1845). For 21 years he held a leading position as a Whig in Parliament. He served as First Lord of the Admiralty and when Fox died he was appointed Secretary for Foreign Affairs. From 1830-34 Grey served as Prime Minister, during which time the Reform Bill (1832) was passed. Although he resigned over some minor changes in a bill concerning the Irish question, the actual cause was months of dissatisfaction with the lack of solidarity and internal friction within the Whig party. Many of his colleagues felt that no Whig government could survive without him, but he gave his support to his successor, Lord Melbourne. When King William IV dismissed Melbourne in November of the same year the Tories returned for five months, but after several defeats the King again asked Grey to form a government. He refused and Melbourne resumed the office of Prime Minister. Actively opposed, however, to the compromises that Melbourne felt impelled to make with the Radicals, Grey became increasingly critical of the administration. Although he continued to play a strong role in the

wings he refused to take official office again (see note 112).

5 'Lady Georgiana Grey (1801-1900), sister of Lady Durham and fourth daughter of Charles, 2nd Earl Grey and Countess Grey.

6 'Lady Louisa Elizabeth Lambton, Countess of Durham (1797-1841). Eldest daughter of Charles, 2nd Earl Grey and Countess Grey and second wife (married 1816) of John George Lambton, 1st Earl of Durham. She bore him two sons, Charles William (1818-1831) who died of tuberculosis, and George Frederick D'Arcy (1828-1879) (note 31), and three daughters, Mary Louisa (1819-1898) (note 7), Emily Augusta (1823-1886) (note 88) and Alice Anne Caroline (1831-1907) (note 15). Lady Durham survived her husband by only sixteen months and died while on a visit to Genoa, Italy.

7 'Lady Mary Louisa Lambton (1819-1898). Eldest daughter of Lord and Lady Durham. Married 1846 (his second wife) James, 8th Earl of Elgin, Governor General of British North America 1846-1854.

8 'Sir William Charles Ross RA (1794-1860). One of the most fashionable English miniature painters of the time.

9 'Sir George Grey, Bart. (1799-1852). Cousin of Lady Durham. Chancellor of the Duchy of Lancaster (1841) in Melbourne's second Cabinet.

10 '°Edward ("Bear") Ellice (1781-1863). Third son of Alexander Ellice and Anne Russell. Married 1807 Lady Hannah Althea (d. 1832), younger daughter of Charles, 1st Earl Grey, and was therefore an uncle by marriage of Lady Durham. He had one son, Edward (note 11), Private Secretary to Lord Durham on his Canadian Mission. "Bear" Ellice was a highly influential member of the Whig party: MP for Coventry from 1818, appointed Secretary to the Treasury and Whip in Lord Grey's government in 1830, and Secretary at War with a seat in the Cabinet in 1833—a position he held till 1834. In 1836 he became one of the founders of the Reform Club, as he had been closely associated drawing up the Reform Bill of 1832. Though he held no official office after leaving the Cabinet, he remained active in politics until his death. He probably knew more about

Canada than any other person in politics in England and his influence upon Lord Durham cannot be overestimated. His father had bought huge tracts of land in North America and in 1803 Edward had come to Canada where he joined John Richardson (a cousin by marriage) in Montreal. He was among those responsible for the amalgamation of several fur trading companies with the Hudson's Bay Company, in which he had large interests. By 1838 he still had land holdings of several hundred thousand acres in the northern US and Canada. The most important was his seigniory of Beauharnois, southwest of Montreal (note 67). It was largely for this reason that he persuaded Lord Durham to take his son on the official staff of the Mission, thereby giving him the opportunity to inspect the family property and deal with problems arising from it.

¹¹"Edward Ellice, the Younger (1810-1880). Only son of "Bear" Ellice (note 10) and Lady Hannah Althea Grey, daughter of Charles, 1st Earl Grey. He and Lady Durham were therefore first cousins. Married Katherine Jane (note 12), second daughter of General Robert Balfour, 6th Laird of Balbirnie. She died in 1864. For 42 years Edward was MP for St. Andrews. In 1859 he became Deputy Governor of the Hudson's Bay Company. In 1838 he came with Lord Durham as his Private Secretary on the Canadian Mission. After Lord Durham's resignation and return to England in November, Edward Ellice with his wife, Jane, and sister-in-law, Tina, went to the family seigniory at Beauharnois. On 3 November Edward was taken prisoner by French Canadian rebels and removed into the bush, while Jane and Tina, together with other British settlers and their anti-rebel supporters, were kept captive in the Curé's house (note 116).

¹²Katherine Jane Ellice (d. 1864). Wife of Edward Ellice, the Younger (note 11). Second daughter of General Robert Balfour, 6th Laird of Balbirnie. For the benefit of her father-in-law, Edward Ellice (note 10) she wrote a perceptive and entertaining diary of the family's experiences on the Canadian visit (*The Diary of Jane Ellice*, edited by Patricial Godsell [Ottawa: Oberon, 1975].) The diary, which reveals her engaging personality, gives an account of their travels across the Atlantic, within

Canada and also a detailed description of a journey to Washington and back by various modes of transport. She also tells of their terrifying experiences when she, her husband and her sister were taken prisoner by French Canadian rebels.

13 [13]Probably George Ponsonby, a moderate Whig politician and colleague of Lord Grey.

14 [14]Lady Caroline Barrington (née Grey), (1799-1875). Lady Durham's sister and third daughter of Charles, 2nd Earl Grey and Countess Grey. Widow of the Hon. George Barrington, Capt. RN (d. 1835).

15 [15]Lady Alice Anne Caroline Lambton (1831-1907). Youngest daughter of Lord and Lady Durham. Married 1853 (his second wife) Sholto John, 18th Earl of Morton.

16 [16]A reference to the circumstances that had brought about the tensions in Upper and Lower Canada, which culminated in the uprising of 1837 (note 2), and the unsatisfactory way with which they had been dealt. This consisted chiefly in the discrepancy between Lord Gosford's conciliatory attitude toward the French Canadians in Lower Canada, and the obvious intention of the British government to continue its traditional controls through the Governor and his selected Councils, as shown by the methods used by Sir Francis Bond Head in Upper Canada. The antagonistic attitude of the British merchants toward the French added a further racial factor to the problems. When hostilities broke out in Lower Canada, Lord Gosford declared martial law. The situation became inflamed and Sir John Colborne, Commander in Chief British forces, had to take strong measures. Unfortunately this led to considerable looting and pillaging by local British volunteers drawn from among the settlers and encouraged yet more ethnic hatred. But it was rationalized to be the result of the murder of a British officer by the French. (See also note 133 on similar measures taken during the 1838 uprising).

17 [17]In 1834 a fire seriously damaged the original Chateau Haldimand (built in 1784). After its repair it was renamed the Chateau St. Louis and was used by the Governors for receptions and balls. During the Durham regime it became the centre of Quebec's social life. The Chateau Frontenac now occupies the

site.

[18]Presumably refers to Capt. the Hon. Henry-Cavendish Grey (1814-1880), Lady Durham's brother and seventh surviving son of Charles, 2nd Earl Grey and Countess Grey.

[19]Col. the Hon. Charles Grey (1804-1870). Lady Durham's brother and second son of Charles, 2nd Earl Grey and Countess Grey. Served as his father's Private Secretary when he was Prime Minister. Offered post as Military Secretary to Lord Durham in 1838 but his father advised him to refuse as he feared personal and political complications on account of Durham's difficult temperament (note 112). Charles Grey was posted to Canada as Officer Commanding the 71st Highland Regt. in April 1838. He carried out Lord Durham's special mission to Washington in June 1838 to ease tensions between the two governments (note 58). He accompanied Lord and Lady Durham to Upper Canada in July and, in command of his regiment, took part in suppressing the rebellion in Lower Canada after Lord Durham's return to England (note 117). In 1837 he had been appointed Equerry-in-Waiting to Queen Victoria, and from 1849-1861 was Private Secretary to Prince Albert. After the Prince's death he remained as Private Secretary to the Queen. He married Caroline Elizabeth Farquhar (note 37). His second son, Albert Henry George became 4th Earl Grey when his uncle died in 1894.

[20]Family name of Charles, 2nd Earl Grey. Lady Durham always referred to her parents by their given names in her letters to them, which was even more unusual at that time than it is today.

[21]Lady Durham was appointed a Lady of the Bedchamber to Queen Victoria in August 1837. She resigned in December 1838 after Lord Durham relinquished his position as Governor-General of British North America and received an official disapprobation from the Queen for issuing his Proclamation defending his case.

[22]Lord Henry Howick, 2nd Viscount (1802-1894). Lady Durham's brother and eldest son of Charles, 2nd Earl Grey and Countess Grey. He became 3rd Earl Grey on his father's death in 1845. In Melbourne's first Cabinet (1834) he was Secretary at War, and held the same post in the second Cabinet from April

1835–September 1839 when he resigned in a reshuffle of Ministers and after a series of disagreements with Lord Melbourne. Married Maria, daughter of Sir Joseph Copley Bart., but as there were no children of this marriage the Grey title passed to the second son of Col. Charles Grey in 1894.

[23]The London home of Lord and Lady Durham.

[24]The Hon. Frederick William Grey (1805-1878) third son of Charles, 2nd Earl Grey and Countess Grey.

[25]Probably either John Fleming (Commander 1814) or Richard Howell (Commander 1816).

[26]Probably Admiral Philip Charles Durham, but despite the surname, this was unlikely to have been a relative of Lord Durham, whose family name was Lambton.

[27]The Hon. Duncombe Pleydell-Bouverie. Second son of the 2nd Earl of Radnor. Admiral Superintendent at Portsmouth 1837--1842.

[28](Lord and Lady Durham), Lord George Lambton, Ladies Mary, Emily and Alice Lambton, Mr. Edward Ellice (Private Secretary), Mrs. Ellice, Miss Balfour, Mr. Turton (Legal Advisor), Mr. Charles Buller (Chief Secretary), Mr. Arthur Buller (Commissioner of Inquiry into Education), Mr. Gervase Bushe (Attaché to Lord Durham), Mr. Edward Pleydell-Bouverie (Attaché to Lord Durham), Lt. Col. George Couper (Military Secretary), Sir John Doratt (Private Physician to Lord Durham), Mr. Saddler (Tutor), Mr. Coke Smythe (Drawing Master). And as ADC to Lord Durham: Lt. the Hon. Frederick Villiers, Ensign William Cavendish, Capt. William Ponsonby, Cornet the Hon. Constantine Dillon, Lt. Stephen Conroy, Lt. Robert Clifford. Another of Lord Durham's staff joined them in Canada a few weeks later, although he is not mentioned by Lady Durham in her journal or letters. Edward Gibbon Wakefield (1796-1842), next to Charles Buller (note 33) was Lord Durham's most important advisor on his Mission. An expert economist on the problems of the colonies, he had been selected by Durham for his exceptional ability. Unfortunately, like Thomas Turton, Durham's legal advisor (see note 32), there had been a personal scandal earlier in Wakefield's life. He had eloped

with a young and wealthy schoolgirl, whom he persuaded to marry him under false pretences. For this he was imprisoned for three years in England, and the marriage was dissolved by a special Act of Parliament. When released he was ostracized by society but worked hard, though anonymously, on various far-reaching theories concerning the organization of land holdings in the colonies. In 1833 he founded the South Australia Association in collaboration with Charles Buller. They actually formed the colony of South Australia on the basis of organized emigration and land sales, and forbade the "dumping" of convicts. Wakefield was ousted because of his record but subsequently organized the New Zealand Association on the same sound principles. Durham, who respected his vision and efforts, intended to appoint him as Commissioner of Crown Lands and Immigration, but because of the problems he had over the Turton case (see note 32) he avoided a direct confrontation with the government and named Charles Buller to the position, although Wakefield did the majority of the work in this field. In 1853 Wakefield emigrated to New Zealand.

[29] Eglantine Charlotte Louisa Balfour, known as Tina (d. 1907). Third daughter of Gen. Robert Balfour, 6th Laird of Balbirnie. In 1853 she married Robert Ellice, son of General Robert Ellice, the younger brother of Edward "Bear" Ellice (note 95).

[30] Captain Francis Erskine Loch. Appointed Captain of the *Hastings* 1838.

[31] Lord George Frederick D'Arcy Lambton (1828-1879). Eldest surviving son of Lord and Lady Durham. Married 1854 Lady Beatrix Hamilton. Lord George Lambton became the 2nd Earl of Durham on the death of his father in 1840.

[32] Thomas Edward Mitchell Turton (1790-1854). Only son of Sir Thomas Turton, Bart. of Starborough Castle, Surrey. Chosen and appointed by Lord Durham as Legal Advisor to the Mission, although this was violently opposed by Lord Melbourne and members of his Government. Unfortunately, some years before, Turton had been involved in a widely publicized scandal in which his wife had sued him for divorce and named her sister as co-respondent. Although Turton later led an exemplary life,

held a senior legal position in India, and was even Church-warden of Calcutta Cathedral, Melbourne and his advisors were outraged at the suggestion of his appointment as a member of Durham's staff. On April 9th Melbourne wrote to Durham: "Turton's was not a common case. It will injure both you and the Government" (L. MSS). Durham remained adamant however, partly because he was a man noted for his unfailing loyalty to his friends, and partly because he was convinced of Turton's exceptional ability. When the Government refused to make the official appointment, Durham offered to pay his salary himself, but Turton refused and insisted on contributing his services voluntarily. From all the evidence available he proved a valuable and highly respected member of the Mission. Col. Charles Grey (note 19) wrote in a letter to his father dated 20 October, 1838 that Turton was "out of sight the best man Lambton has about him" (G.P. See also Lady Durham's comments in her letter of 16 June). Nevertheless Turton's appointment proved to be a source of constant trouble, even to becoming a contributary factor in the final break between Durham and the government. This relentless attitude was certainly hypocritical (even conceding opposition attacks on Turton), particularly when seen in the light of Melbourne's own involvements with married women, however innocent, as he claimed, they may have been. He narrowly avoided personal disgrace in two legal actions brought against him by irate husbands: that of Lady Branden in 1828, and in the more notorious case of 1836 after he became Prime Minister, of Caroline Norton. Although he was officially cleared in both cases, he continued to pay Lady Branden £1000 a year for the rest of her life. Caroline Norton paid more dearly for her indiscretions which cost her her marriage, her reputation and separation from her children. These affairs, and those of others, were obviously in Durham's mind when, after constant harassment on the Turton subject, he wrote to Lord Glenelg, Secretary for War and the Colonies, on 30 July. ". . . You will allow me, my lord, to say that I also on my part have observed with 'great surprise and regret' the tone which Her Majesty's Government adopted in the debates in the House of Lords to which you refer me. Whilst the highest situations in the Empire have been, and still are, held by those who have had the mis-ortune to be convicted of adultery—it is most unjust to denounce and devote to destruction the holder of a petty office, merely because he is wihout political friends or family influence. I feel 'surprise and regret' that Her Majesty's Government did not, at the outset, expose the hypocrisy of this proceeding, and ascribe it to its true cause—the desire to embarrass political opponents, and not a regard for that morality which had repeatedly been violated without compunction or remonstrance" (L. MSS). The whole question of the Turton affair can, in fact, be seen in retrospect as a remarkable microcosm of the larger issue that led to Durham's downfall. Although this was masked in terms of legality, and couched in words of self-righteous indignation and the call of "morality," its sole purpose was political, with the added satisfaction of destroying a personal enemy.

33 [33]Charles Buller (1806-1848). Chief Secretary to Lord Durham and his closest advisor on the Mission. (See Appendix: *Sketch of Lord Durham's Mission to Canada in* 1838, and also Buller's letters to Lord Durham, p. 187 and to John Stuart Mill pp. 172, 185). Son of an official in the East India Company, he entered Parliament in 1830 and was admitted to the Bar in the following year. From the start of his political career he was a radical who strongly supported Lord Durham's leadership of the Reform movement. He was noted in the House of Commons for his wit and his sharp mind, but in private he appears to have had a genial and kind-hearted nature. Although he seems to have been generally popular he was not liked by Col. Charles Grey who wrote to his father on 20 October: "He is clever certainly, but he is weak and vacillating to a degree, and, like all his class of Politicians, unpractical and tricky" (G. P.). However, upon Buller's death, only ten years after the Mission to Canada, both Macaulay and Carlyle wrote of him in moving terms.

34 [34]Lower Canada's House of Assembly had been using a wing of the Bishop's Palace but, now that the House was temporarily suspended, the quarters were being prepared for Lord Durham and his family.

35 [35] Lt. Col. George Couper, 92nd Highland Regt. Military Secretary to Lord Durham 1838. Formerly ADC to Lord Dalhousie and Military Secretary to Sir James Kempt, both former Governors of Lower Canada.

36 [36] 71st Regt. Highland Light Infantry.

37 [37] Caroline Elizabeth Grey (1814-1890), wife of Col. Charles Grey and eldest daughter of Sir T. Harvie Farquhar. Extra Bedchamber Woman to the Queen. Her second son, Albert Henry George (1851-1917) became 4th Earl Grey.

38 [38] Edward Pleydell-Bouverie (1818-1889). Attaché to Lord Durham 1838. Second son of the 3rd Earl of Radnor.

39 [39] One of several indications that Lady Durham's journal, though probably based on a rough draft, was completed in retrospect.

40 [40] See note 17.

41 [41] Commander Henry John Worth. In 1838 he was appointed to the *Hastings* to serve under Captain Loch (note 30).

42 [42] Lady Mary Wood, née Grey, (1807-1884). Lady Durham's sister. Fifth daughter of Charles, 2nd Earl Grey and Countess Grey. Wife of Charles, 1st Viscount Halifax.

43 [43] General Sir Henry George Grey, brother of Charles, 2nd Earl Grey. Lady Grey was the only daughter of Sir Charles des Voeux.

44 [44] Born in 1778, created 1st Baron Seaton in 1839. Commander in Chief of the forces during the rebellions of 1837 and 1838 and also during Durham's term of office. After Lord Durham's resignation Colborne was asked to stay on and assume the additional responsibility of the office of Governor General until the arrival of Charles Poulett Thomson, Durham's successor. In his earlier army career Sir John Colborne had distinguished himself at Corunna and later, under Wellington, at Waterloo, where he was credited with a decisive action in the battle. He died in 1863.

45 [45] While the House of Assembly was being prepared for Lord Durham and his family, they stayed at the Globe Hotel, Quebec.

46 [46] A few hours after the Durham party arrived at Quebec a Canadian steamer, the *Sir Robert Peel*, on its way from Prescott to Toronto, stopped on the American side of the river to pick up wood. A number of armed men attacked it, turned out the passen-

gers and set the ship on fire. One of the ringleaders, Bill Johnson, was from Upper Canada but had joined with American sympathizers to the Canadian rebel cause to raid the shores of the St. Lawrence. This action was not an isolated incident. For some months rebel-refugees and American sympathizers had been quite openly collecting arms, planning raids and even invasion. Although the American Government was not assisting these efforts little attempt was made to stop them. Durham took a firm line from the start. He issued a handsome reward for the capture of the pirates, increased the naval forces on the Great Lakes and the St. Lawrence and arranged for his brother-in-law, Colonel Charles Grey to be sent on a special mission to Washington (See note 58).

47 "Archibald Acheson, 2nd Earl Gosford (1776-1849). Lord Durham's predecessor as Governor of Lower Canada. He was also appointed High Commissioner of a Royal Commission sent to Canada in 1835 to inquire into the nature and to put an end to the continual crises there. Gosford was conciliatory towards the *Patriotes*, which caused considerable criticism. He resigned on 14 November, 1837, a few days before the rebellion. Gosford opposed the Act of Union of 1840.

48 "Sir John Doratt MD. Medical advisor to Lord Durham 1838. Appointed as Inspector General of Hospitals, and of all medical, charitable and literary institutions in the colony of Lower Canada.

49 "The following is an article from the *Commercial Advertiser* dated Quebec, 14 June, 1838: "I availed myself of my worthy friend Mrs. W's invitation to accompany her and her daughter to the Countess of Durham's first drawing-room. Notice was given in all the papers as to the mode of procedure, and I confess I was pleased at the opportunity thus offered of attending the court of a Vice Queen. Nine o'clock was the hour appointed. A guard of honor was drawn up near the entrance of the Chateau, as also a number of police. The carriages had all to fall, in regular order. An Aide-de-Camp in the splendid, indeed if I may say gorgeous, attire of the royal guards, received us at the door, and we passed forward to where another Aide-de-Camp was in

attendance, to whom I handed Mrs. W's card. We were then passed into the large ball room, which soon became filled with ladies and gentlemen. Among the latter were a great number of military and naval officers, many of them covered with stars and different orders. The ladies and gentlemen did not separate, as we do in New York, nor yet stand still, but mingled together, exchanging kindly greetings and cheerful conversation. There were no chairs in the room. On entering the presence chamber we saw a tall and elegant lady standing out from a group which formed a kind of half circle, her station being about two yards in advance. Near her stood the Aide-de-Camp, splendidly dressed, to whom I handed Mrs. W.'s card, as directed, while she made her bow. I also made mine, and she her second, and then taking my arm, we passed on. The Earl was standing alone, almost two yards from the Countess, and to him I bowed, which was returned, and on we went. The operation of passing through the room did not take up more than three minutes, or perhaps two. The whole presentation was over in a little more than an hour. We passed to the hall and back to the ball room, and after some conversation with various acquaintances, we passed down to the saloon, along each side and one end of which, full six feet from the wall, stood a broad elevated table, about four feet high, covered with fruit, ices, lemonade and various liqueurs, wines, coffee, &c. &c. The attendants were inside, and had free range, while the company stood all along, every one receiving what he wished. Thus we amused ourselves for a short time, when we commenced to retreat. No carriage was allowed to leave the stand until called for; and the first called quickly drew up, so that perfect order and regularity pervaded the entire arrival and departure, and all was over within two hours. I'm told nothing like the splendour of the dinner was ever seen. A gentleman who was favoured with an invitation, stated to me that the hour named on the card is six, at which time all are expected to assemble. The guests are received on the stairs by a number of servants, in grand liveries. A servant on the landing requests your name, which is given, and the person in waiting calls it out to the servant on the next landing, who repeats it on your arrival, so that the Aide-de-Camp at the drawing room door hears the name, and presents you to his Lordship, who stands in the middle of the floor. The ladies are presented to the Countess. The kindness of manner and ease with which all are greeted are truly gratifying. Our ladies in New York sit while their company bow, but not so the Countess. She stands up, holds out her hand, and at once you are at ease. Dinner being announced, the Earl takes a lady and precedes the Countess, who follows after the ladies. I should observe that the Aide-de-Camp tells each gentleman what lady he is to hand down, and each gentleman sits beside the lady he so leads to the dinner table. The table is laid for forty each day. The service is of gold, and a splendid row of massive gold cups is laid on each side of the table, within range of the plates, and instead of meats, &c. the table presents only the dessert, with flowers, &c, &c. Not a particle of meat is on the table. A decanter of water, a finger glass half filled, a tumbler or champagne glass, and three wine glasses are on the right of each plate, as also is salt. Servants attend, offering you soup, others with wine, &c. You do not ask for any thing, but take or reject what is offered. No healths are drunk, nor is there any taking wine, not even with the lady you handed to the room. The servants who supply the wine do not fill until your glass is empty, so that you have not to ask, but when he comes forward you state the kind of wine you choose. The banquet continued until nine o'clock, nearly three hours. The servants then filled the glasses. The Earl rose, and all followed his example. "The Queen" was given. All then resumed their seats and in three or four minutes all rose, the gentlemen leading back the ladies to the drawing room, where were coffee, liqueurs and music. The harp, piano, and songs by the ladies, concluded a banquet which, for elegance, ease and pleasure, my friend assured me it would be difficult to surpass. I thought of our loaded tables in New York, and could not hesitate where to give the preference."

[50] Sir Charles Paget (1778-1839). Fifth son of Henry Paget, Earl of Uxbridge. Commanded the North American and West Indian station, an area of the British Navy's world command, until his death on 27 January, 1839.

⁵¹⁵¹See note 46.

⁵²⁵²The Colonial Office.

⁵³⁵³This episode was the most delicate of all the challenges that awaited Lord Durham on his arrival in Canada. Tragically, however, it became the cause of his downfall, although his solution was greeted with general satisfaction by all factions in Canada and, at the time, by the Prime Minister and Durham's own colleagues in Britain. Many people, in fact, considered it a stroke of diplomatic genius to arrive at any kind of acceptable solution. (See Introduction p. 12 for a general outline of the problem.) The following is a short extract from Lord Durham's Proclamation of 9 October, 1838, in which he gave his explanation for his course of action. For the reference to "an acknowledgement of guilt" by the ringleaders of the rebellion see note 60. "The disposal of the political prisoners was from the first a matter foreign to my mission. With a view to the more easy attainment of the great objects contemplated, that question ought to have been settled before my arrival. But as it was essential to my plans for the future tranquillity and improvement of the colony, that I should commence by allaying actual irritation, I had in the first place to determine the fate of those who were under prosecution, and to provide for the present security of the Province by removing the most dangerous disturbers of its peace. For these ends the ordinary tribunals, as a recent trial has clearly shewn, afforded me no means. Judicial proceedings would only have agitated the public mind afresh—would have put in evidence the sympathy of a large portion of the people with rebellion—and would have given to the disaffected generally a fresh assurance of impunity for political guilt. An acquittal in the face of the clearest evidence, which I am justified in having anticipated as inevitable, would have set the immediate leaders of the insurrection at liberty, absolved from crime, and exalted in the eyes of their deluded countrymen, as the innocent victims of an unjust imprisonment, and a vindictive charge. I looked on these as mischiefs which I was bound to avert by the utmost exercise of the powers entrusted to me. I could not, without trial and conviction, take any measures of a purely penal character; but I

169

thought myself justified in availing myself of an acknowledgement of guilt, and adopting measures of precaution against a small number of the most culpable or most dangerous of the accused. To all the rest I extended a complete amnesty (Quebec *Gazette*, 10 October, 1838).

54 [54]Alexander Macdonnell (1762-1840), Bishop of Kingston, Upper Canada. Born in Glen Urquhart, Scotland, where he organized the Glengarry Fencibles, a Roman Catholic Highland regiment that served in Ireland. When it disbanded Macdonnell obtained grants of land for those who wished to come to the Canadas. He and several hundred Highlanders settled in Glengarry County in Upper Canada in 1804. In the war of 1812 he was chaplain to the Glengarry Light Infantry. He became Bishop of Kingston in 1826 and a member of the Legislative Council of Upper Canada in 1831. He died in Dumfries, Scotland in 1840. Alexandria in Upper Canada was named after him.

55 [55]Major-General Sir James Macdonnell. As a Lt. Col. in the Coldstream Guards he served at Waterloo. He later became a Lt. Gen. in command of the Brigade of Guards, and second in command of HM Forces in Canada under Sir John Colborne.

56 [56]The daughter of Charles Cecil Cope, Earl of Liverpool and wife of Lt. Col. Francis Vernon Harcourt. She was born in 1811 and died in 1877.

57 [57]Lady Durham's niece, daughter of her sister Caroline (note 15).

58 [58]One of Lord Durham's first concerns on his arrival in Canada was to ensure peaceful relations with the Government of the United States, but to protest strongly against the continuing acts of piracy and intrusion on to Canadian soil. As his personal emissary, he sent his brother-in-law, Col. Charles Grey to Mr. Stephen Fox, the British Minister in Washington on 12 June, 1838, to arrange an interview for him with the American President, Martin Van Buren. Col. Grey reported to Lord Durham (22 June, 1838) that: "The President assented to everything I stated most fully, and repeatedly desired me to assure Your Excellency 'in the strongest manner' of the sincere desire of the American Government to preserve the good understanding

existing with England, & that you might reckon upon the fullest co-operation which the means admitted, in any measures, which you might think necessary to adopt for restoring the Peace of the frontier." Col. Grey further added that: "Nothing could be more satisfactory than the manner of both the President and Mr. Poinsett [the Secretary of War]" (D.P.).

59 [59] Probably a reference to Lady Durham's brother and fifth surviving son of Charles, 2nd Earl Grey and Countess Grey, the Hon. John Grey (1812-1895) and his wife.

[60] After receiving the confession of 18 June, which was not considered satisfactory as it was ambiguously worded in terms such as "if there be guilt in high aspirations we confess our guilt and plead guilty," a further confession was sought, and signed on 26 June, 1838. This stated: "My lord, we have some reason to apprehend that the expressions used by us in a letter addressed to your lordship on the 18th instant may appear vague and ambiguous. Our intention, my lord, was distinctly to avow that in the pursuit of objects dear to the mass of our population we took a part that has eventuated in a charge of high treason. We professed our willingness to plead guilty, whereby to avoid the necessity of a trial; and thus to give as far as in our power tranquillity to the country. We again place ourselves at your lordship's discretion and pray that the peace of the country may not be endangered by a trial." The signatories were eight prisoners considered to have been the principal instigators of the uprising in Lower Canada in 1837. Lord Durham and his Special Council —Charles Buller, Col. Couper, Col. Charles Grey, Vice-Admiral Paget and Major-General Macdonnell (note 55)—enacted the Ordinance to banish these eight men to Bermuda on 28 June, 1838—Queen Victoria's coronation day. The Ordinance stated that they were to be subjected "to such restraint . . . as may be needful to prevent their return to this province" and should they return without the permission of the Governor they should be declared guilty of high treason, "and shall, on conviction of being so found at large or coming within the said province without such permission as aforesaid, suffer death accordingly" (D.P.). All the other prisoners, who had not already been

released by Sir John Colborne, with the exception of the murderers of a British officer and a French Canadian supporter, were given full amnesty. Unfortunately—and this was a serious error on the part of Lord Durham and his staff—neither the written confession, nor the specific details of it were forwarded to London. Therefore the Ministers, when attacked in Parliament on the illegality of Durham's action, were not fully equipped to support him as they might have done. Charles Buller himself in a letter to John Stuart Mill of 13 October, 1838 admitted: "At the same time I must own that we have done wrong in not supplying them with better materials of justification than we did. A good full despatch would have prevented all the mischief, but I had no time to write a despatch then. I am not yet become quite a good man of business though very sedulous. And the mere routine work of this confounded office takes up my whole time" (D.P.).

61 Third son of the 6th Duke of Bedford. Born 1792, he entered the House of Commons in 1813, was Paymaster General 1830-34 in Melbourne's first Cabinet and Home Secretary 1835-39 in the second Cabinet, until taking over the post of Secretary for War and the Colonies in September of that year. He became Prime Minister in 1846 and died in 1878. Russell, noted for his role in Catholic Emancipation, and as the proposer of the Reform Bill of 1832, was the Minister who presented the Ten Resolutions for Canada, based upon the recommendations of Lord Gosford's Royal Commission of Inquiry (see note 47). The Commons, apart from the Radicals, supported the proposals, but the effect in Canada was to further incite an already explosive situation that resulted in the resignation of Lord Gosford and the uprising of 1837.

62 The following lively account is given in *The Diary of Jane Ellice* (p. 44): "We went with the Ds to the Convent of the *Ursulines*, who had invited us. All the rooms decorated with white muslin, & wreaths of flowers, & about 100 girls decorated in the same manner, ranged in rows down each side of the room wth. bunches of Nuns between. One of them made a splendid speech about his *Lordship's* condescension in coming to "*this*

Western Wilderness," which concluded by all the girls, (Seven of the *biggest* having guitars) singing a *Welcome*. In every other line there was something about *My Lord* or *My Lady*, & whenever these names were pronounced the whole of the White Muslins made low Curtseys & waved their long white handkerchiefs, which had the effect of an *Aurora Borealis*. Then they acted a very *primitive* little play, composed for the occasion, the finale of which was presenting a crown of Laurel to Ld. D., & of Roses to Ly. D." (25 June, 1838).

[63]Major General John Clitherow, Officer Commanding the Montreal District.

[64]Lieutenant Governor of New Brunswick 1837-41. Born 1778, served as Deputy Adjutant General during the War of 1812, as Lieutenant Governor of Newfoundland 1841-46 and as Lieutenant Governor of Nova Scotia from 1846 until his death in 1852. In his last post he was fortunate to witness the first effects of responsible government in Canada, as it had originally been envisaged by Lord Durham. The final details of the system had been worked out for Nova Scotia by Sir John Harvey and by the Colonial Secretary, Henry, 3rd Earl Grey, eldest brother of Lady Durham. These had been endorsed, and instructions for their implementation were given, by the new Governor General, Lord Elgin, son-in-law of Lord Durham by his marriage to Lady Mary Lambton (note 7) in 1846.

[65]The Grey family estate in Northumberland.

[66]See note 46.

[67]The seigniory of Beauharnois, situated on the south shore of the St. Lawrence west of Montreal, was the property of Edward "Bear" Ellice (note 10). Its proximity to Montreal and to the US border, and the high quality of its farmland on the banks of the St. Lawrence, made it one of the most valuable pieces of land in Lower Canada. The seigniory, which had originally been granted by Louis XV to Charles, Marquis de Beauharnois and to his brother Claude in 1729, was eventually bought by Edward Ellice's father, Alexander, in 1795. Alexander Ellice, who had emigrated from Scotland to New York in 1765, had invested extensively in land in the northern United States and in Canada.

In 1810 it was estimated that he owned approximately 133,970 acres in New England, some 280,000 acres (with about 16,000 adjacent acres) in the seigniory of Beauharnois and considerable acreage in Prince Edward Island. Over and above this he had extensive business and shipping interests in connection with the West Indies. Edward, Alexander's third son, and his principal heir, who was related by marriage to Lord Durham, can thus be understood to have been a highly influential absentee landlord, whose advice in Canadian matters was regularly sought, but could not, in fairness, be said to be entirely impartial (see also notes 10 and 83).

[68] Sir George Arthur (1784-1854) served with distinction in the army. In 1814 he was appointed Lieutenant Governor of British Honduras; in 1824 he was appointed to the same position in Van Dieman's Land and in 1837 he became Lieutenant Governor of Upper Canada, with the military rank and command of a Major-General. Although after Lord Durham's resignation Arthur gave Lord Durham his full support and expressed great indignation at his treatment by the government, there had been some slight friction between the two men towards the end of the summer of 1838. The controversy centred around Durham's insistence on personally intervening in the handling of individual cases of clemency toward prisoners in Upper Canada and, in some cases, of questioning Arthur's decisions. The Executive Council of Upper Canada supported Arthur and pointed out that unpleasant consequences could ensue from such undermining of his authority.

[69] Erected to Gen. Sir Isaac Brock (1769-1812), Commander of the British troops in Upper Canada who defeated the invading American army in 1812. He was killed at Queenston in October 1812 during an American attack. This monument was blown up by the Canadian Patriots in April 1840.

[70] Ensign William Henry Frederick Cavendish, 52nd. Oxfordshire Regt. ADC to Lord Durham 1838. Married 1843 Emily Augusta Lambton, Lord Durham's second daughter (note 88).

[71] Though Smythe came to Canada as drawing master to the Durham family, he may have stayed on after they left. He

painted a series of watercolours (c. 1842) entitled *Sketches in the Canadas*, which he dedicated to Lord Durham. He died in 1867.

[72] Arthur Buller. Younger brother of Charles (note 33). He was appointed Commissioner of Inquiry into Education, and he wrote that part of the *Report* devoted to the subject.

[73] The 43rd Monmouthshire Light Infantry.

[74] The following account appeared in an American newspaper in Buffalo, dated 20 July, 1838, of the dinner given by Lord Durham at Niagara Falls: "Before leaving the Falls, Lord Durham requested Major Young to invite forty American citizens to take dinner with him at the Clifton House, at 4 o'clock, and to join in the festivities of the evening. He regretted very much that he could not make the invitation more general, but the house was so small that he was obliged to limit the number. Through the kindness of the Major, I was put upon the list and included among the number, as were also several ladies. As the invitation was entirely unexpected, few if any of us were prepared with any change of clothes—by the help, however, of the barber and bootblack, we brushed up as much as possible, and all things considered, made a tolerable appearance. Punctual to the hour, we went to the Hotel, announced our names, and were shown upstairs. The company consisted of the commissioned officers of the regular army, and the citizens with their wives and daughters, in the neighbourhood. There were few of the Militia officers invited, while there were rather a few invitations given to the Reformers—intimating pretty plainly, that the bigoted and over-bearing course pursued by the ultra Tories, and which has led to all the troubles in the Upper Province, is neither pleasant to him nor to the Government he represents. When dinner was ready, the Earl with the lady of Col. Grey, Sir John Colborne and the Countess, and Lady Mary Lambton, came down to the drawing room, and after a moment's delay to find Major Young, whose arm Lady Mary took, the Earl led the way to the dining room. There was no ceremony observed in seating the guests, except that the Earl took the centre of the table on one side, and the Countess opposite, with Major Young on her right hand, and

between her and Lady Mary. The company at table amounted to about 260. The arrangements of the dinner were no ways different from those of any other general entertainment. The tables were loaded with meats and vegetables, and the guests supplied with a variety of wines very nicely iced, but which nevertheless had a very thawing influence upon the company, for the clatter of knives and forks was soon lost amid the clatter of tongues. The dinner and dessert over, his lordship arose, the company did the same, and he gave "The Queen," which was drank standing. After being seated again, the band of the 43d, which had been playing during the dinner, struck up "God save the King;" and conversation became as general as the general noise would permit. Our glasses being replenished, his Lordship again rose, as did all present, and remarking that he had but one toast more to propose, and in doing so he should take that occasion to express his gratification at seeing their neighbours from the other side mingling so freely with them, and in giving the "President and the United States," he hoped that there would never be any cause for unfriendly collision between the two countries, "and as they were brothers in blood, he trusted they would always remain brothers in sentiment and feeling." This was also drank standing, and to all appearance with hearty good will. We remained at table but a few minutes longer. During dinner, an awning had been spread over the deck roof of a low room now used as a guard room, and thither the company repaired, and such as were strangers were severally introduced to the Earl and Countess—our reception was of the most frank and friendly kind. There was no state, no ceremony, no parade— every thing was easy, and the Earl as familiar as though he had been one of our citizens. After the company had all been presented, they dispersed in groups about the open grounds. As our company were not prepared to stay to the ball, they departed immediately after the presentation was over. When I went to take my leave, I found our noble entertainer, with his family, and Sir John, standing upon the brink of the precipice, overhanging the river and at a point where you have one of the best views of the Falls that can be had on either side, a beautiful bright rainbow was spanning the foaming abyss of the American Fall. Perhaps it was but fancy, yet I thought that he gazed with more than common interest upon that beautiful emblem of mercy and hope, stretching its bright arch oer the troubled waters beneath. As I was alone he detained me a few moments in conversation, expressive of his good feelings towards American citizens, and of his regret that circumstances prevented him from making his entertainment more pleasant. In leaving him I felt that, if I had made the acquaintance of himself and lady, without any knowledge of their rank and station, I should have become strongly attached to them. I could not help turning back and taking one more look at two of the most remarkable men it has been my fortune to come in contact with, one for what he has been, "the fiery old soldier," "the hero of an hundred battles." The other for what he is and will be. Lord Durham has but just commenced his career, and ere it is ended, his name will stand out bright, as one of the benefactors of the human family. The fate of millions rests upon him, and upon his wisdom and prudence, depends the peace and prosperity of two of the finest and greatest nations of the earth. Wisely has the selection been made, for he is of all others the man best fitted for the part he occupies. Liberal and enlightened in his feelings and sentiments, he fully appreciates the position of the country and people he is sent to govern. His mind is of the age in which he lives, enlightened and free. He knows that our example, whether for good or evil is contagious, and that the spirit of enterprise abroad in our own land, and in the Mother Country, must be fastened in the Provinces, and that when men are prosperous, and have ample scope for their energies, they rarely seek to destroy the government which protects them in the enjoyments of the fruits of their enterprising exertions. The course which he is pursuing has disarmed all hostility on this side, and destroyed all sympathy, for if people are not now satisfied they ought to suffer. On the contrary, there is a strong feeling in favour of Lord Durham, and an anxious desire that he may be sustained, for we feel that the misrule of the Tories in the Upper Province is at an end. If there are any more disturbances they will be caused by the Tories, who have become the most bitter opponents to the Governor, because of his clemency and liberal views. The bloodthirsty rascals lament very much that there are to be no more rebels hung. Respectfully yours. . . ."

[75] Sir John Beverley Robinson, Bart., (1791-1863). Second son of Christopher Robinson, noted Canadian editor and publisher. Chief Justice of Upper Canada, 1830-1862. One of the principal members and spokesmen of the Family Compact in Toronto.

[76] See note 46.

[77] The following extracts are from *The Diary of Jane Ellice* (p. 59): ". . . We were to have dined before 5 as Ld. D. wished to go out in the Indian Canoe after dinner, but we did not get back until a ¼ past, which raised his Excely's ire. To revenge himself *he* left us waiting for 20 minutes & did not open his mouth to a soul during dinner. My position in consequence was an enviable *one*. After dinner, though the evening was warm and *lovely*, he said it was too late to go out & would not allow Ly. D. to go. Mrs. Grey, the girls, & all the gentlemen however went off in a fleet of *Canoes*—one Man'd by Iriquois Indians who paddle at an immense pace, singing all the time. Something that sounds like *"Paddy Yaddy,"* "paddy yaddy." Strange wild sounds & wilder looking men—long black hair hanging down their backs; one with scarlet feathers in his ears. They have taken up their position on the *point*, opposite the windows. Some of the gentlemen went to Sup with them. . . . *Ld. D. very ill*—poor man. This is an excuse for his *temper* yesterday. . . . I went in the Indian Canoe with Ld. D. in the evening. He was rather amused at one of the Indians calling the Queen 'The Great English *Squaw.*'" (22/23 July, 1838).

[78] The following is an extract from a letter from Col. Charles Grey to his father, dated 24 July: "Lambton has been very unwell, and consequently very irritable for the last three days. Having nothing to do with him he is always good-natured to us, but I daily thank my stars that I *have* nothing to do with him. It is astonishing, taking everything of importance as coolly as he does, to observe how trifles upset him. With it all however, he is very good-natured to those about him, and I think is liked by

them all, in spite of his *occasional* bursts" (G.P.).

[79] [70]General Samuel Houston (1793-1863). Appointed Commander in Chief Texas Army, 1836. First President, Republic of Texas 1836-38, third President 1841-44, Governor of Texas 1859-61. Deposed because he refused to take the Oath of Allegiance to the Confederate States of America, 18 March, 1861.

[80] [80]Probably Maj. General Robert Patterson (1792-1881). Army officer and industrialist. Presidential elector twice. As Major General commanded the Volunteers.

[81] [81]Captain Henry Bagot (b. 1810). Second son of the Right Rev. the Hon. Richard Bagot, Bishop of Oxford, and Lady Harriet, youngest daughter of the 4th Earl of Jersey. First cousin of Lord Durham. Captain Bagot acted as Secretary to his uncle, Sir Charles Bagot, a staunch Tory and career diplomat, who was Governor General of Canada from 1841-43.

[82] [82]Lady Durham's personal maid who, on account of poor health, did not go to Canada, to the sorrow of both of them. She is mentioned again in one of the final letters as she embarks on a new role in her life.

[83] [83]Though Edward Ellice, the Younger (note 11) was an official member of Lord Durham's entourage, his father, "Bear" Ellice, had obviously manœuvred him into his position of Private Secretary for the main purpose of carrying out various family business matters while he was in Canada. Much of this was connected with the seigniory of Beauharnois (note 67) where the Ellices spent much of their time. The family also owned large tracts of land in the northern US and from 19 August to 26 September they travelled to Washington and back via Niagara. As they did not accompany the Durham party on their visit to Upper Canada during July, the total length of time that Edward spent with Lord Durham must have been minimal.

[84] [84]Lt. the Hon. Frederick Child Villiers (1815-71) Coldstream Guards. Lord Durham's cousin, third son of the 5th Earl of Jersey. ADC to Lord Durham 1838.

[85] [85]Lt. the Hon. Octavius Duncombe, known as "Tommy", 1st Life Guards. A colourful and controversial figure in his private and public life. He had always been a strong Radical supporter of

Lord Durham. A gentleman jockey, a sensational bankrupt, he was later involved in the presentation of the famous Chartist petition, an action which shocked many who considered Chartists as potential revolutionaries.

[86]Maj. Gen. Sir Colin Campbell (1776-1847). Fifth son of John Campbell of Melfort. Commander of Forces and Lieutenant Governor of Nova Scotia 1834-40. In 1840, despite his popularity, he was asked to resign by the House of Assembly on the grounds that he was averse to Responsible Government.

[87]Sir Charles Augustus FitzRoy (1796-1858). Eldest son of Sir Charles FitzRoy. Lieutenant Governor of Prince Edward Island 1837-41. Married Lady Mary Lennox (1820), daughter of the 4th Duke of Richmond (Governor in Chief of Canada 1818-19).

[88]Lady Emily Augusta Lambton (1823-1886). Second daughter of Lord and Lady Durham. Married 1843 William Henry Frederick Cavenidsh, ADC to Lord Durham 1838.

[89]Sir Charles Paget died five months later on 27 January, 1839.

[90]The Hon. George Grey (1809-1891). Lady Durham's brother and fourth surviving son of Charles, 2nd Earl Grey and Countess Grey.

[91]Captain James Robertson Crauford, 1st Grenadier Guards.

[92]Captain Arthur Wellesley Torrens, 1st Grenadier Guards.

[93]There is little doubt that Lord Brougham's personal animosity towards Lord Durham was the major cause of the latter's downfall, but it would oversimplify the matter to ascribe it to that alone. Lord Henry Peter Brougham, Baron Brougham and Vaux (1778-1868) was a brilliant man of great learning and eloquence who brought all the skills of his legal profession to the aid of his ambition and vanity. In his youth he and Durham had been close friends and allies on the subject of parliamentary reform, but Brougham played his hand cautiously enough to keep himself in favour with the more moderate, right wing members of the Whig party. When Melbourne formed his first Cabinet in July 1834, Brougham was appointed Lord Chancellor. However in the heated debates on the Reform Bill, Brougham was a strong supporter of the radical wing and the bill was passed in 1832. The problems in Ireland—religious discrimination, economic

hardships and taxation inequities, all leading to increasing racial friction—were the next major challenge facing Melbourne's government. The King (William IV), angered by the passing of the Reform Bill, was incensed at the thought of compromising with the Radicals over the Irish question. Brougham, whose self importance led him to behave as if he were Prime Minister, brought the government into direct conflict with the King. This rift, which also split the Whig party, finally led to King William dismissing Melbourne and his government. A Tory government, under Sir Robert Peel, was hastily put together, and to the disgust of his colleagues Lord Brougham offered his services (at a reduced salary!) Peel's government, however, was defeated again and again in the House of Commons and Melbourne was once more back in power in April 1835. In the formation of his second Cabinet he dropped Brougham. By the time William IV died in 1837, Brougham realized that his exclusion from office was not due to the King alone and he turned his full vehemence upon attacking the government in the House of Lords. Lord Aberdeen said of him: "Nothing can equal Lord Brougham's hatred and contempt of the government, which he now shows on every occasion. He is determined at all hazards to do his utmost to turn them out" (A/L Corr., I. 96). Lord Brougham's attack upon Lord Durham's Ordinance was, therefore, a two-edged weapon with which he was able to attack his former friend, and, at the same time, the Whig government which he ostensibly served. Yet, oddly enough, despite his infidelity, he retained the close friendship of Lord Melbourne that he had had all his life, and on Melbourne's death was one of the executors of his estate. But for Lord Durham, Melbourne had hardly ever a good word.

94 "Daniel O'Connell (1775-1847). One of Ireland's national heroes, nicknamed The Liberator. In 1823 he founded the Catholic Association with the aim of claiming the right of parliamentary representation for Roman Catholics. Although as a Catholic he could not take his seat in the House of Commons, O'Connell was elected MP for Co. Clare with a massive majority in a by-election in 1828, thus forcing the government to grant Catholic emancipation in 1829. Although he co-operated with

the Whigs to obtain any advantages he could for Ireland until 1841, he then launched his campaign for the repeal of the union.

95"General Robert Ellice (1784-1858). Younger brother of Edward "Bear" Ellice (note 10). His eldest son Robert married Jane Ellice's sister, Eglantine (Tina) Balfour (note 29) in 1853.

96"Melbourne to Durham, 28 July: "I received per bag your letter of the 30th ult. yesterday morning & hastened to give yours and Ldy. Durham's letters to the Queen. Her Majesty was much gratified by them both, & has desired me to tell you so. H.M. will write to Ldy. Durham herself. I am much obliged to you for what you have written to me (about the ordinance) which is most distinct, clear & satisfactory. I have not time to do more than acknowledge it. Indeed I have nothing to express but the most entire approval and concurrence. I am very happy to hear that you have settled the very difficult affair of the Prisoners & settled it so well. We must deal with them as best we can at Bermuda. I understand some difficulties may be apprehended. Your ordinance will have no validity nor confer any power there. [This would suggest that Durham's Commission *did* give him the validity and power to act as he did in Canada and banish the prisoners, but that in Bermuda there was not, at that time, the legal process to retain the prisoners there. See also extract from Durham's Proclamation, note 109.] You are quite right in making use of your present power to introduce as many good laws as you can. There can be no doubt of the feeling of satisfaction that prevails in the province. It must be like a sudden transition from the discord of Hell to the peace of Heaven. A strength which at once puts down all parties is naturally agreeable to all. Make a constitution, but for God's sake make one that has a chance of working. All colonial assemblies, it appears to me, are always resisting to the extreme of their power, and if they do this, they necessarily further their own destruction. Affairs must go on, and if they cannot go on with the assembly they necessarily proceed without them [Responsible government, as proposed by Lord Durham, did in fact achieve this object.] Adieu! My Dear Durham. Remember me to Lady Durham and believe me yours faithfully, Melbourne" (L. MSS.).

"Glenelg to Lord Durham, 31 July, 1838: "I write a few un-
official lines to express the pleasure we feel in receiving your
Despatch of the 29th June transmitting your proceedings regard-
ing the prisoners. The course you have taken is in consonance
with the wishes expressed in my communications with you & Sir
J. Colborne. You will see by the papers that our old enemies
attacked your ordinance proclamation last night. These attacks
are after all impotent in this country. I trust they may be equally
harmless in the colony. All reasonable people here approve your
conduct. My colleagues and I entirely approve—our opinion is
that, altho' there may be some legal inaccuracies of form, the substance is entirely right & the result satisfactory. You have solved
a very difficult question most judiciously & ably, in a way at once
most merciful & just & equally grateful to most parties & impartial judges—& on the confidence which I hear on all sides, all
classes in Canada repose in you. Go on & prosper. Parlt. will soon
be up, & your measures will not have this running fire to meet. . . .
Glenelg" (D.P.).

⁹⁸The Queen to Lady Durham, 31 July, 1838: "Tho' I have
written to you, but a very few days ago, I cannot refrain from
again doing so, to thank you for your letter of the 29th June, and
for all the kind expressions it contains for which I feel very
thankful. Pray be so kind, my dear Lady Durham, as to convey
to Lord Durham my sincere thanks for his kind letter, which
gave me much satisfaction [This comment refers to the personal
letter written by Lord Durham to the Queen offering his congratulations on the occasion of her coronation in which he expressed his regret at not being there in person but: ". . . I can only
console myself by laying at your Majesty's feet, from America,
the best tribute of loyal respect and devotion that I can offer . . .
I have been able to do this (the amnesty) in your Majesty's name
without danger, because I have in my own done all that sound
policy required in the way of punishment and security. Not one
drop of blood has been shed. The guilty have received justice,
the misguided mercy; but at the same time, security is afforded
to the loyal and peaceable subjects of this hitherto distracted
province . . ."]. You will have I suppose, heard by this time how

well everything went off at the Coronation and what marks of affection and loyalty I received from, I may say, the whole nation. It was a proud day for me, and one which I shall ever remember with gratitude. With my best love to your daughters and Mrs. Grey, believe me always, my dear Lady Durham, yours affectionately, Victoria R" (L. MSS.).

[99] [99]The following announcement appeared in the Quebec *Gazette* of Wednesday, 19 September, 1838: "New York *Commercial Advertiser*: Mr. Hall of the above newspaper arrived in Quebec (5 p.m. Sept. 19th) with news, dating to Aug. 13th, which arrived in New York on the packet ship *Wellington* of the debate in the House of Lords on the Ordinance. The banishment to the Bermudas etc. is declared illegal. Lord Melbourne said that he should advise the Queen not to sanction the ordinance of the Earl of Durham." The complete account of the disallowance was contained in the paper.

[100] [100]Although all the Canadian newspapers carried accounts of these proceedings the complete details are recorded in the Quebec *Gazette* beginning on Friday, 21 September, 1838 under the section "Imperial Parliament . . . House of Lords, Aug. 7. Canadian Affairs."

[101] [101]With the exception of those extremists who were actually in the process of planning the second rebellion, all factions and newspapers in Upper and Lower Canada united in support of Lord Durham. The French Canadian newspaper, *Le Populaire*, commenting on Durham's ordinance, stated that: "the only act that was practicable, the only act which could have sheltered the greater number by inflicting a light punishment on the few, is declared null and void." *Le Canadien*, the leading French Canadian newspaper, said: "The proceedings of the House of Lords have thrown all classes of society into a turmoil of anxiety, of which our history, fertile in events palpitating with interest, can offer few parallels. Every one can feel, touch, see, the disastrous consequences which have been prepared in Canada by noble Lords sitting tranquilly in their comfortable senatorial chairs, who have transformed the Canadian question into a plaything or weapon of party . . ."

The question of Lord Durham's resignation was, and by some historians still is, a subject of controversy. In Canada, and amongst Canadians generally, the opinion was that he should remain. The three Lieutenant Governors urged him to stay; most of the newspapers did the same, and public meetings were held in towns and many villages petitioning him not to leave. But those who worked closely with him felt otherwise. Col. Couper, Sir John Colborne and Sir James Macdonnell all agreed that his only option was to resign. Even the government in London anticipated his resignation and wrote asking Sir John Colborne to extend his tour of duty. Of those who felt he should return to England, some thought he could do more for the Canadian cause by being in London (and had he not returned when he did the *Report* might never have been written, as he did not live much longer), but there were others who felt that his health and psychological state of mind were no longer able to sustain the strain. Charles Grey wrote to his father on 30 September saying: "For himself I would not advise him to stay. I really think it would kill him. I never knew a man so affected by the attacks upon him both in Parliament and the newspapers [in England] and his mind works upon his body to a degree that is quite fearful" (G.P.). But a letter of even greater perception perhaps is that written by Charles Buller to John Stuart Mill on Saturday, 13 October, 1838: ". . . The truth is that Lord Durham's health and character utterly unfit him for such a service as the one he is now on. He would do it better than any other of our public men, because he is thoroughly honest, and has larger and better views than any of them. But he is so anxious and so nervous that he literally cannot bear the burden of *distant responsibility*. In the interval of suspense before the news came he was in such a state of dejection that he would for some time do nothing himself, nor let me do anything. I was in despair; and though by sharp remonstrance I induced him to go rightly, I was thoroughly convinced that the sooner he could get out of the matter with honour the better for him and his friends. In his place I as Governor Genl. would not have resigned. But I thought it best he should. I thought it was a good pretext for his doing what I only wanted a pretext for his doing. I, in his place would have gone on just as he did before, legislated boldly and trusted to the very check I had just received for frightening the imbeciles who offered it to me. But he would not have gone on boldly. He has plenty of boldness—boldness of an admirable kind. But he has no *constancy*. How can a man whose whole frame is bedevilled by liver and rheumatism be steady and firm? The effect of this in his case would have been that he would have thrown himself on the British party [the British mercantile group in Canada] and made himself more or less their tool. My sympathies for the Canadians are not a bit diminished. Justice to them—the great majority—is still my first principle. But believe this they can do nothing for themselves: they have no habits of self-reliance: their friends must serve them without leaning on them. Woe to the man who trusts to their energy or prudence in their own cause. Hence every man who governs here, the moment he ceases to rely solely on himself is either bullied by the British, who have great energy and tact, or throws himself on them. Lord Durham would have done the last. With his character it was inevitable. Rather than he should do so it was better he should resign: and if he failed, fail without fault of his own. Had Lord D. stayed he would have failed. I think therefore that it was a great thing to get him away when the blame would rest on others. The only question is whether the circumstances justify him in doing *what he has determined to do* . . . [with] his Special Council to make the changes in the civil law of the country, which must be made in order to ensure future tranquillity, after the re-establishment of representative government. . . . Prepare a scheme for the future settlement of this country. This he will do: this is all that is left for him to do. You will observe therefore that he says in the Proclamation that while he abandons the hope of doing any good by continuing to act as *Governor*, he will still complete his task as High Commissioner. He will report on the State of Canada: report on the *mode* by which tranquillity can be restored and maintained. He does not therefore fling up his Mission abruptly: he does not return with his task uncompleted" (D.P.). The subject of Durham's failing health is prominent in this letter but there is also the implication that under stress Durham had, by nature, a tendency to lose confidence in himself. This point is also evident in another extraordinary letter written by Buller to Durham himself at an earlier date (7 September, 1838), even before his knowledge of the disallowance of the ordinance. Even then Durham was starting to lose heart and threatening to resign because of the constant attacks made upon him by his critics in Parliament and in the British newspapers. Buller's intention at this time was to strengthen Durham's resolve to ignore his enemies. "Day after day I have gone to you with the intention of making you acquainted with the view of affairs which all those, who have your interests most at heart, concur in taking and expressing among one, another; and every time I have been turned away from my purpose either by that despair of the ultimate success of your mission, which now frequently crosses me and makes me refrain from what I consider fruitless labour, or by getting alarmed at the effect which what I said seemed to have produced on your health. I will not, however, without an effort deliberately abandon myself to the former of these feelings: and an attempt must be made even at the hazard of temporary injury to your health, to rouse you from a state which threatens the worst consequences not only to your health, but to your reputation and happiness. I am the less tender of your health because no-one can have observed you without seeing that, be your bodily disorders what they may, the real cause of sufferings is in your mind, and from that you have no chance of recovery without raising yourself from your present morbid state of feeling. I should be wanting in the first duty of a friendship which, believe me, though of recent date is very true and very strong, were I not to make an exertion to save you from a catastrophe, after which I believe in my conscience that you and your best friends will attach little value to the preservation of your health or even your life. You will think this exaggerated language ... You seem to think that if not properly supported at home and here, you have nothing to do but resign, and vindicate yourself by proving the withdrawal of the confidence which you regard as essential to your success ... But I think you must have had proof enough by this time of the utter ignorance of the public at home as to the affairs of Canada. They know nothing of the real nature of your difficulties; nothing of the causes which render the want of support, of which you have reason to complain, peculiarly embarrassing . . . You have undertaken, in time of danger, the maintenance of one of the most exposed defences of the Empire. The post was entrusted to you simply from the general confidence in you as the only person capable of maintaining it. Why then do you suddenly abandon the post of honour and of danger? You cannot do this without accounting for it to most severe judges. And in proportion to the high hopes which a nation has formed of you, and the high trust which it has reposed in you, will be the fearful recoil of its unexpected disappointment, and the terrible downfall which you will experience from the noblest position ever occupied by any public man in England since the first Pitt. You have followed no ordinary path to fame and power. You have courted those high and daring enterprises, which end in triumph or political death. You have been attacked by the Tories. Did you ever expect anything else? You—who have been without any exception their deadliest enemy, who gave them the most fatal blow they ever experienced [the passing of the Reform Bill], and have ever held them up in the most unqualified language to public scorn and reprobation. Depend upon it, the Tories hate you more than any man in England, because you have given them the most reason to hate and fear you. They will do everything to damage and ruin you in public estimation. It is natural that they should do so. Everybody anticipated it; almost everybody expected you to triumph over it. . . . The Ministers have not given you the support you have the right to expect. They have betrayed you. [The question of the validity of the Ordinance had not yet come up. This comment refers to lack of governmental support for Durham: constant criticism about the extravagance of the Mission, the appointment of Turton, etc.] But you will get little sympathy in England if you urge this as a mischief, which you did not foresee. Nobody ever imagined they had any love for you. Every one regards you as the most formidable rival or rather actual competitor that they have to dread. . . . Your line is to produce good measures in perfect assurance that they will produce good feelings and ensure you that amount of public confidence which may be necessary to give those measures a fair trial. This is the line you took when, instead of throwing yourself into the hands of a party, you composed your Executive and Special Councils of persons representing no will but your own. By so doing you declared your intention of pursuing your own course careless of the opinion of parties here. This system has perfectly succeeded, as yet; all parties have acquiesced in it or rather approved of it. . . . But what is the dissatisfaction expressed towards you? Till within a month ago, you had every proof from every party, if not of confidence, at least of as confiding a disposition as the circumstances permitted. What public manifestations have you had of a contrary feeling? Nothing but the mere mercenary and insane blackguardism of a press which represents no one and guides no one. The people of England gave you despotic power because they thought you had courage, wisdom and justice enough to use it for this people's benefit, in spite of this people itself. And they will hardly believe that such a power has proved inadequate in consequence of the impertinences and slander of one penny and two half penny papers. My opinion is that the reasons which you regard as justifying failure or withdrawal from your charge will not be considered sufficient. . . . Imagine, for your imagination is fruitful in that line, taunts from the public press to which those which have hitherto produced an effect on you that I cannot comprehend, will have been mere trifles. Picture to yourself the delight with which you will be regarded by Ld. Brougham and Sir James Graham, the torture of having to be thankful for an exculpation by Ld. Glenelg, and the ignominy of being spoken of in the same category with Ld. Gosford. Here you must conquer success in spite of the government and the opposition at home. You are Governor General—you have your Special Council for Lower Canada. These are your means of saving yourself, and saving yourself by a success which will send you home incontestably the most powerful public man in England. . . . It is perfectly obvious that a most unfavourable change has been

189

produced in public feeling in these provinces by the late debates in Parliament [on Turton and the formation of the Executive and Special Councils] and the inference that is naturally being drawn from them that you are not strong enough at home to carry your own policy into effect. . . . This effect you foresaw to be inevitable from the moment you read these debates. Your part was by all possible means to counteract this impression by showing yourself utterly unmoved, by allowing no abatement of courage or cheerfulness to attract public attention, by rather displaying increased energy and devotion to your great task. You have done exactly the reverse. You have allowed yourself to be more influenced by these debates than any are in the Province; you have formed an apparent determination to fret yourself until the next despatches arrive; in the meantime you feed yourself on anything next most harassing that comes in your way and worry yourself by reading blackguard attacks in the newspapers, and imagining even worse as likely to assail you hereafter; so that at last anxiety and mortification combined have acted so on your body as to produce your present state of health, and just now, when your presence in public was most wanted, keep you at home or allow you to appear only as an invalid. This unfortunately has produced the worst results. In this little town everybody speculates on your state and movements. Some exaggerate your bad health and represent you as in a very alarming state; others say that you are yourself making the most of your illness in order to have a pretext for going home. . . . While there is even a chance of your remaining you must not act so as to mar your future policy. While you retain the title, do not abandon the functions of Governor General. Above all, I implore you, as I value your comfort, your dignity and your freedom of action, to pay no attention to the press. It cannot serve you either by guiding or warning you; its only effect is that of irritating; and that you can obviate by simply not reading any papers, in which you expect to find anything offensive. . . . I have explained my views and feelings at great length. I have expressed them in a language of plainness—even of roughness to which you have not been accustomed from your friends, and which your first impression will be that I have no right to use towards you. But I know that you have too much justice, too much generosity to mistake the feeling which has prompted me to use it. I report to you the substance of what all your friends, all who have made your interests their own, say in speaking of you; and which it is but just that one of them should say in speaking to you" (D.P.).

[103] Josephine Clifton (1813-1847). The first American actress to appear in a starring role in London in *Bianca Visconti*.

[104] With no Christian names given it is impossible to determine the connection between this gentleman and the famous Charles Greville whose *Greville Memoirs* 1817-60 are of such interest on this period.

[105] This took place in a number of towns including Quebec and Toronto. The following description is of the occasion in Montreal, reported in the Montreal *Herald* of 4 October, 1838: "Two transparencies, each six feet by nine, were mounted on a transparent coffin, borne by pall bearers, who carried lighted torches. On the coffin the word *Brougham* was painted. One of the transparencies represented Lord Brougham seated on a jackass, with his face to the animal's tail, an imp of darkness leading the ass and exclaiming 'Come along, old boy!' while his Lordship says 'I protest against the legality of this ordinance;' 'Protest and be d——d.' A fingerpost, stuck up at a short distance, having on it the words *Road to Hell*. The other transparency represents his Satanic Majesty as having fastened a cord around the necks of the three Lords (Brougham, Melbourne and Glenelg), and hauling them up to their appointed place, very much against their will. His Majesty says, 'No mistake, you must come.' These two transparencies form the two sides of a box, on the ends of which is painted, 'Thus may the ends of British interests perish.' . . . Lord Brougham and his noble fellow traitors were publicly hanged and burned in effigy, amid the cheers of thousands. . . . We had almost forgot to mention that Lord Glenelg was represented as asleep."

[106] Durham waited until he had received the official notification of the disallowance of the ordinance from Lord Glenelg on Saturday, 26 September before sending his official resignation. In a

private letter to Lord Glenelg he said: "I am bound to tell you privately that I never could have anticipated the possibility of such treatment as I have received. Having succeeded, far beyond my most sanguine hopes, in restoring tranquillity and inspiring confidence, all over the Continent of North America, I little expected the reward I have received from home—disavowal and condemnation. . . . In these circumstances I have no business here. My authority is gone—all that rests is military power, that can be better wielded by a soldier, and Sir John Colborne will, no doubt, do it efficiently. I shall appear in Parliament not to defend my conduct, for it needs no excuse, but to expose the cruelty, injustice, and impolicy of those who have trifled with the best interests of these Colonies for purposes of personal enmity or party hostility" (Q series PAC).

[107]Born in France in 1796, Quiblier entered the Sulpician order and was sent to Canada in 1825. He became the Superior of the Seminary in Montreal and is generally regarded as the principal organizer of primary education among French Roman Catholics in Montreal. He died in 1852.

[108]Robert Barnwell Rhett (1800-1876). Senator and Congressman.

[109]Lord Durham's Proclamation in its entirety appeared in all the leading newspapers, but for ease of reference in Canada it can be found in the Quebec *Gazette* of Wednesday, 10 October, 1838. It is a document that has caused great controversy. Durham's intention was first of all to calm the angry, and in some cases dangerous, reaction towards Britain and Melbourne's Government. Rebellion was imminent, due to what Canadians felt was a total lack of concern for the colonies for the sake of British party politics. It was even becoming difficult to raise volunteer troops to support the regular British army forces, who were equally outraged by the disallowance of the ordinance. Second, Durham felt justified in explaining why he had taken the action he had and under what authority. He is quoted by the Quebec *Gazette* (10 October, 1838) as saying, "I did not accept the Government of British North America, without duly considering the nature of the task which I imposed on myself, or the sufficiency

of my means for performing it. When Parliament concentrated all legislative and executive power in Lower Canada in the same hands, it established an authority, which, in the strictest sense of the word, was despotic. This authority Her Majesty was graciously pleased to delegate to me. I did not shrink from assuming the awful responsibility of power thus freed from constitutional restraints, in the hope, that by exercising it with justice, with mildness, and with vigour, I might secure the happiness of all classes of the people, and facilitate the speedy and permanent restoration of their liberties. But I never was weak enough to imagine that the forms by which men's rights are wisely guarded in that country where freedom has been longest enjoyed, best understood, and most prudently exercised, could be scrupulously observed in a society almost entirely disorganized by misrule and dissension. I conceived it to be one of the chief advantages of my position, that I was enabled to pursue the great ends of substantial justice and sound policy, free and unfettered. Nor did I ever dream of applying the theory or the practice of the British Constitution, to a country whose constitution was suspended— where all representative government was annihilated, and the people deprived of all control over their own affairs—where the ordinary guarantees of personal rights had been in abeyance during a long subjection to Martial Law, and a continued suspension of the Habeas Corpus—where there neither did exist, nor had for a long time existed, any confidence in the impartial administration of justice in any political case." English-speaking Canadians received the Proclamation with praise and congratulations. In other quarters, however, it was the cause of such dismay and outrage that the reputation of Lord Durham has always suffered as a result of it. One small paragraph in the Proclamation was the forerunner of many others in like vein in the *Report* that have led to Lord Durham being considered one of the French Canadians' greatest enemies—the person they hold originally responsible for undermining their national aspirations. "To encourage and stimulate me in my arduous task, I had great and worthy objects in view. My aim was to elevate the Province of Lower Canada to a thoroughly British character, to link its

people to the sovereignty of Britain, by making them all partici-
pators in those high privileges, conducive at once to freedom and
order, which have long been the glory of Englishmen. I hoped
to confer on a united people, a more extensive enjoyment of free
and responsible government, and to merge the petty jealousies
of a small community, and the odious annimosities of origin, in
the higher feelings of a nobler and more comprehensive nation-
ality." In later paragraphs he openly chided his own government
for not supporting him as they could have done. His facts were,
of course, correct, but to state them publicly in his own defence
while still a personal representative of the Queen and her government was considered unspeakable by many people in Britain
and caused him to receive the official disapprobation of the
Queen. However, most of the Radicals, and a good proportion
of the general public, supported him and seriously considered the
possibility of his replacing Melbourne in a show of strength. But
on his return to England Durham made no attempt to challenge
Melbourne and devoted himself to the preparation of the *Report*: "The particular defect in the Ordinance which has been
made the ground of its disallowance was occasioned, not by my
mistaking the extent of my powers, but by my reliance on the
readiness of Parliament to supply their insufficiency in case of
need. For the purpose of relieving the prisoners from all apprehensions of being treated as ordinary convicts, and the loyal inhabitants of the Province from the dread of their immediate
return, words were inserted in the Ordinance respecting the disposal of them in Bermuda, which were known to be inoperative.
I was perfectly aware that my powers extended to landing the
prisoners on the shores of Bermuda, but no further. I knew that
they could not be forcibly detained in that island without the
cooperation of the Imperial Legislature. That cooperation I had
a right to expect, because the course I was pursuing was pointed
out in numerous Acts of the Imperial and Provincial Legisla-
tures, as I shall have occasion hereafter most fully to prove. I
also did believe that, even if I had not the precedents of these
Acts of Parliament, a Government and a Legislature anxious for
the peace of this unhappy country and for the integrity of the

British Empire, would not sacrifice to a petty technicality the vast benefits which my entire policy promised and had already in a great measure secured. I trusted they would take care that a great and beneficent purpose should not be frustrated by any error, if error there was, which they could rectify, or the want of any power which they could supply; finally, that if they found the Ordinance inoperative they would give it effect—if illegal, that they would make it law. This small aid has not been extended to me, even for this great object; and the usefulness of my delegated power expires with the loss of that support from the supreme authority which could alone sustain it. The measure now annulled was but a part of a large system of measures, which I promised when I proclaimed the amnesty. When I sought to obliterate the traces of recent discord, I pledged myself to remove its causes— to prevent the revival of a contest between hostile races—to raise the defective institutions of Lower Canada, to the level of British civilization and freedom—to remove all impediments to the course of British enterprize in this Province, and promote coloni- zation and improvement in the others—and to consolidate these general benefits on the strong and permanent basis of a free, responsible, and comprehensive government. Such large prom- ises could not have been ventured, without a perfect reliance on the unhesitating aid of the supreme authorities. Of what avail are the purposes and promises of a delegated power whose acts are not respected by the authority from which it proceeds? With what confidence can I invite cooperation, or impose forbearance, whilst I touch ancient laws and habits, as well as deep-rooted abuses, with the weakened hands that have ineffectually essayed but a little more than the ordinary vigour of the police of trou- bled times?" (Quebec *Gazette*, 10 October, 1838).

[110]See note 93 on Lord Brougham.

[111]Lt. Stephen Rowley Conroy, Coldstream Guards. ADC to Lord Durham 1838.

[112]Unfortunately Earl Grey did not think Lord Durham's Proc- lamation satisfactory. Although both he and Col. Charles Grey, who wrote to him on the subject from Canada, felt that the gov- ernment had treated Durham in a very "shabby" manner over

the ordinance and defended him hotly, Earl Grey was appalled by the Proclamation. On 29 November he wrote to his son saying: "All the faults of his character from which I always feared that it would turn out unfortunately for himself, his family, and the country, seem to have broken out at last with a violence proportionate to the control which he seems previously to have held them" (G. of H. MSS). Earl Grey had never liked or trusted his son-in-law whose extreme Radical views he deplored. When the possibility arose of Col. Charles Grey becoming a permanent member of Lord Durham's Mission, Earl Grey wrote to him on 4 July, 1838 saying: "I foresaw from the beginning the probability of much difficulty in the new arrangements and therefore was anxious that you should stick to your Regiment, your proper place, the duties of which would furnish a sufficient excuse for declining any employment Lambton might propose to you" (G. of H. MSS). Grey had not even been anxious for his son to undertake the Special Delegation to Washington and felt this should have been done through the normal official channels. To be fair, Lord Durham had earned and provoked his father-in-law's dislike of him when, in the earlier years of the Reform Bill debates, Durham had bitterly, and even viciously attacked him on a number of occasions. At the time of one of these, Lord Melbourne commented that, "if I had been Lord Grey I would have knocked him arse over head" (G.J., II, 266). Yet, strangely enough, Durham did respect his father-in-law. Lady Durham recounts in her journal of the last days of Durham's life that: ". . . he felt himself under no obligation to any one living but Papa. From him he had received his Earldom, & the Red Ribbon, which had been the free gift of the late King, not proposed by any of the Ministers, but owing, as he believed, to Papa's observations to Sir Herbert Taylor. He had been very anxious at the beginning of the year that Papa should come to town & not hold himself so completely aloof in all that was going on. He thought that if a change of Govt. took place, he was the only person with whom there was a chance of any good" (L. MSS.). On another occasion Lady Durham said: ". . . he told me he wished his Red Ribbon to be returned to the Queen by Papa

—as a mark of his respect and his affection for him" (L. MSS.).

[113]Although actual violence did not break out until two days after Lord Durham's departure, it had been evident for several weeks that it was imminent. Sir John Colborne had prepared to meet it, but his preventive measures were complicated by the fact that most of the preparations for the insurrection in Lower Canada were taking place south of the border. In Upper Canada plans to rebel were also under way. Although in both Provinces this situation had been a continual threat, the disallowance of the Ordinance, indicating lack of support for the government in Canada and therefore its consequent weakness, evidently acted as a great encouragement to the rebels.

[114]Andrew Stevenson (1784-1857). Congressman and diplomat. Appointed US Minister to Great Britain 1834.

[115]Cornet, the Hon. Constantine Augustus Dillon (1813-1853), 7th Dragoon Guards. Fourth son of Henry, 13th Viscount Dillon. ADC to Lord Durham 1838.

[116]But, in fact, on 28 October, four days before the Durham party left Canada, the Ellices went back to Beauharnois. On the night of 3 November armed rebels attacked the seigniory taking Edward and the other male occupants into the bush as prisoners, and keeping Jane and her sister Tina under guard in the house. A vivid account of their experiences is given in *The Diary of Jane Ellice.*

[117]Although the uprising began at Beauharnois, where the village was destroyed, it was soon re-taken and occupied by the 71st Regiment under the command of Col. Charles Grey. The rebels established their headquarters at Napierville, near the US border, with a force of about 2000-3000 *Patriotes*. Because of the neutrality agreement made with the American government they were, however, poorly armed. Sir John Colborne, with a force of about 5000-6000 men consisting of regular British troops, together with volunteers and Indians, advanced upon them and they scattered. Minor outbreaks occurred in other areas, but as martial law had been declared on 4 November the rebellion was soon under control.

[118]Captain Daniel Pring RN. Commanded the *Inconstant.*

197

[119]3rd Marquis. An extreme Tory reactionary.

[120]See also Charles Buller's *Sketch of Lord Durham's Mission to Canada in* 1838 (Appendix) for a moving account of Lord Durham's departure.

[121]Captain Robert Lambert Baynes. Commanded the *Andromache* from February 1838 to 1843.

[122]Presumably one of these ladies was Lady Elizabeth Bulteel née Grey (1798-1880) Lady Durham's sister, second daughter of Charles, 2nd Earl Grey and wife of John Croker Bulteel.

[123]Lt. General Lord Rowland Hill, 1st Viscount Hill (1772-1842). Commander in Chief 1828-1842.

[124]From the time of his arrival in London on 7 December Lord Durham had worked continuously on the preparation of his report, with hardly a moment's break, even over Christmas. Although some preparatory work had been done in Canada most of it was written in England. As Charles Buller, his Chief Secretary, did not return from Canada until 22 December, the pressure upon Lord Durham after his recent experiences, and in his rapidly declining state of health, must have been considerable. The *Report* was finally signed on 31 January, 1839 and presented to the Colonial Office on 4 February. Parliament met the following day. Although some parts of the document had been obtained and printed by *The Times* on 8 February, which caused a somewhat complex scandal resulting in the "resignation" of Lord Glenelg as Colonial Secretary, the *Report* in its entirety was laid before the House on 11 February.

[125]Lord Glenelg was succeeded by the Marquess of Normanby who held the position until September, when it was taken over by Lord John Russell (see note 61).

[126]Lord James Archibald Stuart-Wortley-Mackenzie, 1st Baron Wharncliffe (1776-1845). Represented Yorkshire in Parliament for several years. Created a peer in 1826.

[127]Lord William Forward, 4th Earl of Wicklow (1788-1869). A representative peer for Ireland. Lord Lieutenant for County Wicklow.

[128]Lord George William, 10th Earl of Winchelsea (1791-1858).

[129]On 3 May, 1839 the government announced that it would

introduce legislation to bring about the union of Upper and Lower Canada based on the recommendation made in Lord Durham's *Report*. However there was considerable vacillation on the subject, and a number of modifications were made before it came up for debate some weeks later. The outcome was a proposal to send a Governor to Canada to prepare the way for the Union and to carry out other recommendations made in the *Report*. Responsible government, as outlined by Durham, however, was not accepted at this stage. Under this system the people elect their representatives and a majority form a Ministry, which is responsible to Parliament. A Ministry resigns if it loses the confidence of the parliamentary majority. Any Governor appointed by the British government would not have been permitted to overrule the Canadian Parliament. Thus Canadians would have been free to govern themselves on matters of Canadian concern. Durham's recommendation, however, was predicated upon a Union of Upper and Lower Canada, as he was unwilling to permit the French Canadians any form of complete autonomy.

130 Charles Poulett Thomson (1799-1841). Created 1st Baron Sydenham of Sydenham and Toronto in 1839 and remained there until he died in 1841 after a fall from a horse. Unlike many former Governors he was not a member of the aristocracy. Son of a merchant, he was a successful businessman himself, before being elected MP for Manchester. In Melbourne's second Cabinet he was President of the Board of Trade. While he was Governor General, the Union Act that united Upper and Lower Canada and established the Province of Canada, was passed on 23 July, 1840, four days before Lord Durham died in England. The Act, however, differed in some important respects from Durham's proposals, the most vital being that it gave equal representation to both Provinces—an injustice to Lower Canada with its larger population—which Durham had not intended.

131 Jane Ellice and her sister Tina were rescued by the 71st Regiment and a large contingent of volunteers on the night of 10 November after they, and about 60 other people, had been kept prisoner for a week by the rebels in the curés house. On the

199

following evening, Edward and the other men taken prisoner were also rescued.

[132]Col. Grey and some of his regiment remained at Beauharnois after rescuing the Ellices.

[133]Sir John Colborne declared martial law at the outbreak of insurrection on 4 November. Large scale attacks were made on the rebels by combined regular and volunteer troops. Many of the latter lost all reasonable control of themselves and Col. Grey, in his journal and letters to his father, spoke in horror of the excesses: "I cannot bear to see the poor wretches of women and children when their husbands etc. etc. are dragged away by the Volunteers, and in many cases their houses burnt over their heads. . . . Thank Heaven, I have had nothing to do with any burning." On 13 November he wrote: "Col. Fraser, who commands the Glengarrys [local Volunteers] says they are looked upon as savages, to which I could not help answering that I thought by his own account they rather deserved it" (G.P.). Colborne took 753 prisoners. 108 were court martialled and 99 condemned to death, though only twelve were executed. 58 were deported to Australian penal colonies, two banished and 28 freed on bond for good behaviour.

[134]Canadian rebels who had fled over the border.

[135]After a terrible storm at sea on their return from New York, in which their sailing ship could have been wrecked, they arrived in England on 15 December.

[136]See notes 96 and 97.

[137]*Sketch of Lord Durham's Mission to Canada.* P.A.C. Durham Papers, No. 23, Vol. 1.

INDEX

The numbers given below refer to the footnotes. Principal biographical information is given in the note indicated by the use of guillemets.